A VOICE OF REFORM

A VOICE OF REFORM

Essays By

TAT'IANA I. ZASLAVSKAIA

Edited with an introduction by
Murray Yanowitch

M. E. Sharpe
Armonk, New York   London, England

Copyright © 1989 by M. E. Sharpe, Inc.
80 Business Park Drive, Armonk, New York 10504.

Available in the United Kingdom and Europe from M. E. Sharpe,
Publishers, 3 Henrietta Street, London WC2E 8LU.

Library of Congress Cataloging-in-Publication Data

Zaslavskaia, T. I.
    [Selections, English. 1989]
    A voice of reform : essays / by Tat'iana I. Zaslavskaia ; Murray
Yanowitch editor.
       p.   cm.
    Translated from Russian.
    Includes index.
    ISBN 0-87332-505-2
    1. Soviet Union—Social conditions—1970– 2. Soviet Union—
Social policy. 3. Soviet Union—Economic policy—1986–
 I. Yanowitch, Murray. II. Title.

HN523.5.Z368213 1989
306'.0947—dc19   88–23802
                                             CIP

Printed in the United States of America

CONTENTS

INTRODUCTION

The Influence of Tat'iana I. Zaslavskaia on Soviet Social Thought

Murray Yanowitch

It has become common, both in Soviet and in Western writings about the USSR, to characterize the early 1980s (the immediate pre-Gorbachev period) as years of "stagnation" or, at the very least, "near-stagnation" in the Soviet system. Whatever the justification for applying this characterization to the Soviet economy, it is not always recognized that this same period was a time of considerable intellectual ferment in the Soviet social science literature. On close inspection, it is clear that the apparently sudden outburst of reformist thinking since 1985 is actually an elaboration and reinforcement of concepts and ideas that had already begun to emerge in the pre-Gorbachev years. We are by no means suggesting that there is nothing strikingly new about Soviet economic and social thought in more recent years; but we are pointing to a certain continuity within Soviet reformist intellectual discourse that pre-dates the Gorbachev period. The writings of Tat'iana I. Zaslavskaia, trained as an economist and today one of the most influential and best known Soviet sociologists, provide an illustration of this proposition.

In a 1984 essay on economic sociology, written jointly with Rozalina V. Ryvkina (see selection 2), Zaslavskaia—then the head of the Social Problems Department of an Academy of Sciences institute in Novosibirsk—cited several Soviet colleagues whose recent writings on social and economic themes she regarded as related to her own. Who were these writers, and what was there about their work (other than an interdisciplinary focus) that prompted Zaslavskaia to consider it complementary to her own efforts? The question is worth asking, for even our brief answer will help establish some of the elements of a common reformist intellectual orientation which had begun to take shape in the years of "stagnation," and which obviously has found much fuller expression in the more recent work of Zaslavskaia and her colleagues.

The 1984 article referred to above explicitly cited the work of Boris Kurashvili, Vladimir Iadov, and Vadim Rogovin, among others. The first had argued for a transition from the prevailing "command system of management" to a relatively decentralized "stimulative" system with increased opportunities for "self-management" (Kurashvili, 1982). Similarly, Iadov's studies of work attitudes seemed to suggest that the aspirations fostered by the educational and cultural levels of young workers would remain frustrated unless accompanied by the "democratization of management" (Levin, 1983). Rogovin's writings had begun to pose the issue of implementing "social justice" not only in the economic sphere and in ensuring relatively equal "starting positions" for the offspring of various social groups, but also in access to "the adoption of socially significant decisions" (Rogovin et al., 1982, pp. 7–18). Zaslavskaia also attached "great importance" to studies by Hungarian economists and sociologists of the role of "group interests" in their socialist society. Finally, although she did not cite the work of her sociologist colleague Arkadii Prigozhin, she was certainly aware that his writings on the sociology of organizations had warned against delay in implementing "radical innovations" in management, and had stressed that the "restructuring" of organizational mechanisms could be at least as effective as technological advance in accelerating economic growth (Prigozhin, 1983, p. 6; 1984, pp. 57–67).

This highly compressed summary of the concepts and sentiments which circulated in the reform-minded social science literature of the immediate pre-Gorbachev years suggests the kind of intellectual environment in which Zaslavskaia's essays—at least the early ones collected here—were written. (It also indicates, incidentally, that the new political leadership had at its disposal in the mid-1980s an appropriate vocabulary and conceptual apparatus that could be drawn upon to formulate and introduce its program of "restructuring.") Some of the principal features of the socioeconomic environment of those years, to which her studies were addressed, are well put in Zaslavskaia's own words: "At the end of the 70s and early 80s, in many sectors of the economy, one could observe a noticeable weakening of labor, production and planning discipline, an increase in the turnover of trained personnel, a deterioration in the attitude toward work, the premature breakdown of expensive equipment, irrational expenditures of raw materials and energy'' (Zaslavskaia and Kupriianova, p. 27). Yet all of these negative features could be observed at the same time as the educational, skill, and cultural levels of the workforce continued to increase. This combination of circumstances helps explain why the recurring question which Zaslavskaia so often appears to confront is how to account for the enormous underutilization of the ''labor potential'' (or ''human factor'') in the Soviet system.

What are some of the principal themes in Zaslavskaia's essays and how has she influenced the work of other Soviet sociologists and economists?

Conflicting group interests in Soviet society

By 1984 Zaslavskaia's earlier stress on the need to study the ''social aspects'' and ''social components'' of economic development, and the urgency of promoting the closest ''interfacing'' of economic and sociological research (see selection 1) had become embodied in a newly emerging intellectual discipline or ''scientific current''—economic sociology. Much of her published work since 1984 may be regarded as an effort to legitimate this discipline and demonstrate its usefulness in studying not only the sources of stagnation in the Soviet system but also the obstacles confronting efforts to reform it. The principal focus of Zaslavskaia's economic sociology is the study of economic activity as a ''social process'' involving the interaction of classes, strata, and social groups occupying different positions, endowed with unequal rights and obligations, and guided by distinct—often conflicting—interests. This approach is explicitly intended to encompass not only the formal or ''official'' economic mechanism but the ''shadow'' economy as well, and the interaction between these two sectors.

What is significant about such an approach to the study of the economy and society under Soviet circumstances? Perhaps most challenging to long-established ''official'' views was Zaslavskaia's explicit acceptance of the notion that Soviet society was characterized by conflicts of interest between contending social groups. The importance of adopting such a position can only be appreciated when we recall the unambiguous terms in which the traditional Soviet view was stated. Here is an illustration drawn from an 1968 edition of the Soviet *Philosophical Dictionary* (cited in Ryvkina, 1986, p. 30): ''Under socialism the interests of society objectively become the common interests of all of its members.'' Without denying the existence of common interests

("... in a stable peace on earth, and in conserving the natural environment"), Zaslavskaia's formulation clearly represented a break with these traditional ways of characterizing Soviet society: "However, every social group has its own special interests, which may come into contradiction with the interests of other groups" (see selection 4).

But it is not simply the explicit recognition of conflicts of interest between social groups that merits attention here. Far more important is the "escalating" manner in which this concept has been applied, both by Zaslavskaia and by others. The principal context of her early discussion of group conflict concerned the expected consequences of some projected decentralizing, market-oriented economic reforms. To be successful, any such reforms would necessarily have to reduce the size and authority of administrative strata attached to industrial ministries while increasing the independence and authority of enterprise executives. Such reforms would certainly weaken the former social group and strengthen the latter—a clear conflict-of-interest situation. Hence the need for a "social strategy" that would neutralize the expected efforts of the former group to block such reforms. All of these points were made in Zaslavskaia's writings published in 1985 (see selections 3 and 4).

By 1987 Zaslavskaia was invoking the concept of conflicting group interests in a much broader context. For example, some of the more tragic pages of Soviet history—the "mass repressions" as a case in point—served the "narrow interests" of a "particular social group" at the expense of the interests of the bulk of society. A particularly telling illustration of the potency of this way of thinking about Soviet society is suggested by Zaslavskaia's observation that any shortage—whether "of rights, information, openness, goods or services"—is to some group's advantage (see Interview, pp. 140 ff. in this volume).

But especially intriguing are the policy implications that emerge from Zaslavskaia's discussion of divergent and conflicting group interests. The "contradictory" or conflicting nature of these interests is not something that can be "abolished." The problem is not the existence of such interests but the restricted opportunity which some groups have had to limit the "appetites" and "group egoism" of others. Indeed, for Zaslavskaia, democracy is a state of affairs (not yet available in "excess," she notes) in which all social groups have the right "to express, defend, and implement their own interests." This is clearly the direction in which Soviet society must move, in Zaslavskaia's view (see selection 5 and Interview). Such a formulation seems fully in accord with the notion of "socialist pluralism," which Zaslavskaia does not explicitly cite here but which other Soviet writers have invoked in a similar context (Gordon and Klopov, 1988, p. 31).

By 1987–88 the theme of conflicting group interests had begun to permeate Soviet public discourse. Some of this literature has even sought to demonstrate the emergence of a new managerial-administrative "class" (adherents of this view explicitly stress the "class" nature of this social group) bent on frustrating efforts at any economic reform that threatens its inflated size and power (Andreev, 1988). Other examples of the literature on this general theme have had the more modest aim of reporting on the results of empirical studies of the attitudes of enterprise managers toward specific aspects of projected economic reforms. At least some of these studies have made it clear that there is considerable managerial resistance to proposals for "elections" of managers and other vehicles of "worker participation" (Kiselev and Petrikov, 1987). Whether these and other studies have been directly inspired by Zaslavskaia's work or not, it is clear that her insistence on the critical role of conflicting group interests has paved the way for the comparatively open discussion of what was formerly regarded as a non-problem in Soviet society.

Work attitudes and work behavior

In an essay published early in 1986 Zaslavskaia observed that human labor had become the "weak link in the functioning of sophisticated technological systems" (see selection 5). This remark was clearly not intended as a casual reference to inadequate work skills or to familiar lapses in labor discipline—failings that had been commonly discussed in the Soviet labor literature for decades. Rather, the intention was to focus attention on the increasingly serious problem of deteriorating work morale and work performance. Abundant empirical evidence of this for the early 1980s had emerged in the studies of rural enterprises (both farm and non-farm) conducted by Zaslavskaia and her colleagues at the Institute of the Economics and Organization of Industrial Production (based at the Siberian Branch of the Soviet Academy of Sciences in Novosibirsk) (see Zaslavskaia and Kupriianova, especially ch. 10–13), although the relevant evidence was obviously not confined to this area. What was the justification for characterizing labor as the "weak link," and what was the root of the problem? We shall see in what sense Zaslavskaia's answers—especially to the second part of the question—

constitute a contribution to reformist social and economic thought.

One of the more obvious indicators of the deteriorating situation was the apparent increase in the share of "passive" workers among the employed population. These were workers whose behavior in the production process was guided by the principle "it's no concern of mine." This process was clearly associated with the spread of what Zaslavskaia characterized as an increasingly "instrumental" attitude toward work, with work being regarded as essentially a means for obtaining satisfactions away from the job (the consumption sphere), and the work process itself as inherently less rewarding. A statement summarizing the West Siberian studies conducted by Zaslavskaia and her colleagues in 1980–84 concluded that a principal hypothesis of the research group— namely, that the poor production performance in the area stemmed "above all" from the comparative indifference ("inadequate interest") of workers toward their jobs—was confirmed by the studies' findings (Zaslavskaia and Kupriianova, p. 207). Especially disturbing was the fact that this state of affairs appeared to apply to managerial personnel no less than to ordinary workers and collective farmers.

Little wonder, then, that sociologists like Zaslavskaia and Ryvkina began to explicitly characterize significant portions of the workforce as "alienated" from their work (selections 6 and 8; Ryvkina, 1987). The use of the "alienation" concept in this context was not an incidental rhetorical flourish. For decades Soviet writers had either denied the relevance of the concept to a socialist society, or treated obvious symptoms of it as representing merely "survivals" of the past. In any case, the dominant view had been that "alienation in no way arises from the essence and nature of socialist relations" (Blium, 1987, p. 112). Zaslavskaia and Ryvkina introduced no such qualifications in their affirmation of the concept's relevance to Soviet circumstances. On the contrary, their formulations suggested that the alienation of labor was deeply rooted in the core institutions and practices of the Soviet economy. This was certainly the implication of Ryvkina's references to the "alienation of working people from property" and from "the system within which they functioned." Such alienation was reflected in what Ryvkina characterized as the "indifference toward work, the low level of involvement, the low quality of work and of produced output."

What were the principal sources of these attitudes and the indifferent work performance that accompanied them? What was needed to reverse the situation?

Paradoxically, part of the problem was the continuing improvement in the "social quality" of the workforce—its educational, cultural, and skill levels. This was a more informed and sophisticated workforce than ever before. But the system of economic management at both the macro and micro levels had remained essentially frozen for decades. The critical point stressed by Zaslavskaia was that the more skilled and "socially developed" worker had become less amenable to the traditional methods of "administrative" or "directive" management and the relations between superiors and subordinates associated with these methods: "As people's educational level rises and their general outlook broadens, they strive for a greater degree of independence in their work, for an active part in the decision-making process, and for the unleashing of their own creative potential. If this striving is not realized, people frequently become alienated from work, and turn their interests to other spheres" (selection 6).

The "directive" or "administrative" methods of management permeated relations between superiors and their subordinates all along the organizational hierarchy. The strict supervision and regulation of enterprise management by its superiors (in the ministry or similar government agency) was, in effect, reproduced in the relations between enterprise management and its subordinates (Kiselev and Petrikov, 1987, p. 54). Instead of the delegation of authority from higher to lower levels of the organizational hierarchy, what often prevailed was the opposite process—the "appropriation" of the normal authority of lower levels by the higher ones (Zaslavskaia and Kupriianova, p. 217). This not only helped explain the considerable work discontent Zaslavskaia found among managerial personnel; it also suggested how little genuine decision-making authority remained at the bottom of the hierarchy, among ordinary workers and peasants. As Zaslavskaia observed, if people's work experience persuades them "that initiative is more frequently punished than rewarded, and that obedient, not creative, workers fare better, one can hardly expect active workers to predominate" (selection 5).

In the Marxian vocabulary that continues to be used in these discussions, the problems of work attitudes and indifferent work performance reviewed here reflect the lag of production relations (essentially the relations between managers and managed at all levels of economic organization) behind the comparatively developed state of the productive forces (the human and tangible capital available to society). In this context, Zaslavskaia's stress on the importance of providing increased opportunities for participation in decision-making at the workplace—

opportunities for "self-control" and "self-management"—represents much more than empty sloganeering. These are obviously intended as "practical" measures in response to an urgent problem—the enormous underutilization of the "human factor" in the production process. But such measures also constitute one aspect of the broader democratization process required in the society as a whole.

The theme of "social justice"

A useful way of assessing the significance of Zaslavskaia's writings on the issue of social and economic inequality, or more broadly, on the theme of social justice, is to contrast her views with those of another prominent Soviet sociologist, Mikhail N. Rutkevich. Indeed, some of her discussion of these matters appears to be a critical response to the more-or-less "official" position earlier expressed in the writings of Rutkevich.

In the late 1970s and early 1980s Rutkevich repeatedly elaborated the notion of the increasing "social homogeneity" of Soviet society (Akademiia nauk SSSR, 1976, pp.211–218; Rutkevich, 1980, pp.270–282). Class and strata differences in work content, income, and group interests were presumably declining steadily. The resulting "convergence" in the economic position and general "mode of life" of social groups signified the growing "unity" of Soviet society. Zaslavskaia, on the other hand, has stressed the emergence of new sources of social differentiation, in particular, those arising from inequalities between "hierarchical groups of administrative personnel," between employees of "rich and poor" government departments, between residents of small and large cities, between the working population and pensioners (selection 8). Moreover, her observation that "injustice in distribution" has increased in recent years (1987, p. 36) and has become a principal source of alienation from "social goals and values" (selection 6) suggests a very different state of affairs than Rutkevich's perception of growing "social homogeneity" and "unity."

The contrasting approaches of these sociologists are most strikingly expressed when they confront the issue of obstacles to the further implementation of social justice (the meaning attached to this term will be clarified below). For Rutkevich the principal obstacle to the establishment of social justice "in its full scope" is the comparatively undeveloped state of the "forces of production," i.e., the still inadequate level and abundance of technology and work skills. Hence income must be distributed largely in accordance with work performed ("socialist justice") rather than in accordance with "need." Similarly, the inadequate level of technology (and the resulting inequalities in income and cultural development of families) make it impossible to provide equal opportunities for advanced schooling for the offspring of different social groups. "Complete equality in realizing abilities can be achieved only when conditions of existence are equal, i.e., where there is distribution according to need" (Rutkevich, 1986, p. 16). Hence any significant movement toward social justice "in its full scope" must await the arrival of the communist society of the future.

Zaslavskaia readily acknowledges the limits on equality imposed by the current state of the "productive forces." But there is another factor operating which makes for "incomplete justice" in current Soviet society, namely the unwillingness of certain social groups to give up their "inordinate privileges" voluntarily (selection 5). For Zaslavskaia the main obstacle to distributive justice in the present is the failure to apply consistently the familiar socialist principle of distribution: "From each according to his abilities, to each according to his labor." Nor does its more comprehensive application require a significant leap forward in the level of "productive forces."

What is needed to implement the first portion of the familiar principle? (Zaslavskaia notes that traditional expositions have focused on its second half.) An obvious first step is the provision of more equal "starting conditions" for children raised in families of differing social backgrounds. More specifically, this means increased equality in the provision of high quality pre-school and general-education facilities in different regions, in rural and urban areas, and in cities of different size. The objective here is to ensure greater equality of opportunity in access to advanced schooling and the most preferred occupations. For Zaslavskaia there is an obvious connection between such a policy and the implementation of the principle "from each according to his abilities . . ." But this principle also requires that, once employed, people are allowed to work under conditions that provide sufficient scope for their work abilities. It is here that the freedom-enhancing quality of Zaslavskaia's "broad" interpretation of the familiar socialist principle of distribution comes into play. The principle is violated not only when workers are idled by scarcities of raw materials and spare parts, and managers are "bound hand and foot" by instructions from their superiors, but also when teachers are unable to teach in a manner they consider appropriate, when scholars have their research projects closed down prematurely, and when people in the arts are prevented from performing in a manner justified by their talents. In all of these cases people are forced to work "below their ability" (selection 5).

As for the second part of the socialist principle of distribution (". . . to each according to his labor"), recent Soviet commentary has typically invoked it as a weapon against allegedly widespread wage leveling (*uravnilovka*) or "egalitarianism." But for Zaslavskaia this is a less serious violation of distributive justice (or so it seems, given the scanty attention paid to it in her writings) than certain practices commonly associated with "privileges" for favored social strata. Especially objectionable, in Zaslavskaia's view, is the existence of "closed" channels of distribution for certain goods and services. One of the most persistent themes permeating her discussion of distributive justice is the need to enforce the "equal purchasing power of the ruble" for all social groups, or—put somewhat differently—"the open nature of trade in all types of consumer goods" (selections 5 and 6; Zaslavskaia, 1987, p. 36). Thus her writings in this area have contributed to the recent burgeoning of a substantial literature directed against "privilege" in Soviet society (for other examples see Rogovin, 1986; Naumova and Rogovin, 1987; Malein, 1987).

Perhaps most promising, in the sense of its potential for extending the scope of future Soviet discussions, has been Zaslavskaia's explicit recognition that the socialist principle of distribution (or, for that matter, the communist principle of distribution in accordance with "need") is inadequate as a guide to the implementation of social justice in non-economic spheres of life. At the very least, criteria of justice remain to be elaborated for legal, political, and family relations (selection 8; Zaslavskaia, 1987, p. 36). There is little in Zaslavskaia's own discussion that suggests the precise nature of the appropriate criteria. But some of her comments on the broad theme of social justice suggest the direction that future Soviet discourse in this area might take. "It is unjust when some people make decisions, and other people suffer the consequences if they turn out to be incorrect" (Interview). The critical implications of this formulation for the assessment of the Soviet political system are difficult to avoid.

Another challenging formulation that will have to be confronted in Soviet discussions of prevailing political institutions is Zaslavskaia's observation that social justice is strengthened through a "struggle of interests" in which different social groups can "openly express, discuss, and defend their interests . . ." (selection 5). Is this not an affirmation that "justice" in the political sphere requires the democratization of Soviet political institutions?

Economic versus social goals

The terms "social policy" and "social development" have not always been consistently applied in Soviet discussions; but their usual meanings are reasonably clear. They suggest measures such as improved working and housing conditions, increased supplies of consumer necessities, and more effective educational and training facilities, all of which have been commonly justified on the grounds of their expected positive impact on workers' productive performance. In any case, the usual context—at least until recently—implied the subordination of social policy to economic policy, of social goals to economic goals.

Zaslavskaia seemed to challenge this approach in the early 1980s, although in a somewhat ambiguous manner: "The development of socialism is a process that is not only, and perhaps not so much, economic as it is social" (Zaslavskaia, 1982, p. 10). By the second half of the decade, however, her position was being stated much more directly: Under conditions of economic underdevelopment it is normal for social goals to be subordinated to economic goals, for social policy measures to be regarded essentially as means of increasing society's "economic and production potential." But that time has passed. Economic development, and in particular the "accelerated growth of the productive forces," must now be recognized as a necessary means of attaining social goals, i.e., reduced social inequalities, a more advanced system of "social relations," and the development of "man himself" (selections 5 and 8).

The somewhat rhetorical nature of these formulations should not obscure the fact that something new is being proposed here. This becomes apparent when we consider the kinds of social policy measures that seem appropriate to Zaslavskaia in the present situation (measures that should presumably be regarded as ends in themselves rather than simply as means of improving economic performance). Social policy must not only provide for people's "vital necessities" (its traditional function), but must respond to their needs for "accurate social and political information, political and economic democracy, social respect . . . and intensive intellectual life" (selection 5). Like her remarks on the need to formulate criteria of social justice for areas of "social relations" other than the economy, Zaslavskaia's objective here appears to be to open up new issues for discussion rather than to present a complete statement of her own on the particular topic at hand (in this case, the nature of social policy). That she has been at least partially successful is suggested by the recent appearance of works by other authors that have sought to elaborate the theme of subordinating economic to social policy (Rakitskii, 1988).

Our objective here has not been a comprehensive introduction to the essays included in this volume. Rather we have sought to demonstrate some of the principal ways in which Zaslavskaia's writings have contributed to "reforming" the manner in which Soviet social science literature portrays its own society. At the moment, the author of these essays is President of the Soviet Sociological Association and Director of the newly formed National Public Opinion Research Center, in Moscow. It will be interesting to observe whether her accession to these positions will facilitate the implementation of a principle affirmed in one of her recent essays (selection 7): "The light of sociological research must penetrate into the remotest corners of social life, expose the rubbish that has accumulated, and encourage a prompt and total housecleaning in the home in which we all live." Readers with a scientific interest in Soviet society cannot help but be encouraged.

*   *   *

The editor would like to thank Patricia A. Kolb of M. E. Sharpe, Inc. for her many valuable suggestions at all stages of this project.

References

Akademiia nauk SSSR, Institut sotsiologicheskikh issledovanii (1976). *Sotsial'naia struktura razvitogo sotsialisticheskogo obshchestva v SSSR* (Moscow).

Andreev, S. (1988). Causes and Consequences. In *Ural*, no. 1, pp. 104–139.

Blium, R. N. (1987). Alienation and Socialism. In *Filosofskie nauki*, no. 9, pp. 112–114. [For an English translation see *Soviet Studies in Philosophy*, vol. 27, no. 2.]

Gordon, L. and Klopov, E. (1988). The Thirties and Forties. In *Znanie–sila*, no. 4, pp. 22–31.

Kiselev, S. V. and Petrikov, A. V. (1987). The Innovative Potential of Managers of Agro-Industrial Enterprises. In *Izvestiia sibirskogo otdeleniia akademii nauk SSSR, Seriia ekonomika i prikladnoi sotsiologii*, no. 13, Issue 3, pp. 3–14. [For an English translation see *Problems of Economics*, vol. 31, no. 2.]

Kurashvili, B. P. (1982). State Management of the Economy: Prospects of Development. In *Sovetskoe gosudarstvo i pravo*, no. 6, pp. 38–48.

Levin, M. (1983). Youth and Labor: Reflections of Sociologists and a Journalist. In *EKO*, no. 8, pp. 110–128.

Malein, N. S. (1987). Unearned Income, Justice, Humanism and the Law. In *Sovetskoe gosudarstvo i pravo*, no. 10, pp. 57–63.

Naumova, N. F. and Rogovin, V. Z. (1987). The Task of Justice. In *Sotsiologicheskie issledovaniia*, no. 3, pp. 12–23. [For an English translation see *Soviet Sociology*, vol. 27, no. 1]

Prigozhin, A. I. (1983). *Organizatsii: sistemy i liudi* (Moscow).

Prigozhin, A. I. (1984). Managerial Innovations and Economic Experiments. In *Kommunist*, no. 7, pp. 57–67. [For an English translation see *Problems of Economics*, vol. 27, no. 10.]

Rakitskii, B. V. (1988). Distributive Relations: Principles of Approach and Methods of Analysis. In *Obshchestvennye nauki*, no. 3, pp. 50–63.

Rogovin, V. Z. (1986). Social Justice and the Socialist Distribution of Vital Goods. In *Voprosy filosofii*, no. 9, pp. 3–20. [For an English translation see *Soviet Sociology*, vol. 26, no. 4.]

Rogovin, V. Z. Babin, B. A. and Degtiar', L. S. (1982). *Sotsial'naia spravedlivost' i puti ee realizatsii v sotsial'noi politike* (Moscow).

Rutkevich, M. N. (1980). *Dialektika i sotsiologiia* (Moscow).

Rutkevich, M. N. (1986). Socialist Justice. In *Sotsiologicheskie issledovaniia*, no. 3, pp. 13–23. [For an English translation see *Soviet Sociology*, vol. 26, no. 4.]

Ryvkina, R. V. (1986). Sociology and the Management of Social Processes. In *EKO*, no. 9, pp. 16–34.

Ryvkina, R. V. (1987). Overcoming the Braking Mechanism. In *Sovetskaia Estoniia*, November 11. [For an English translation see *Soviet Sociology*, vol. 27, no. 3.]

Zaslavskaia, T. I. (1982). Interview. In *Znanie–sila*, no. 2, p. 10.

Zaslavskaia, T. I. (1987). The Need for Restructuring is Dictated, Of Course, Not Only by the Economy. In *Nauka i zhizn'*, no. 11, pp. 35–37.

Zaslavskaia, T. I. and Kupriianova, Z .V., editors (1987). *Sotsial'no-ekonomicheskoe razvitie sibirskogo sela* (Novosibirsk).

A VOICE OF REFORM

1 | Economic Behavior and Economic Development

The director of one of the prosperous Western Siberian state farms, a public-minded man, a captain of rural industry, described the experience of mechanized teams that operate without work orders. This form of organization of work is unquestionably progressive and increases labor productivity dramatically because people show a greater degree of responsibility and initiative in their work. As a result, the average earnings (wages) of equipment operators on these teams, based on the results of the year, were 500–600 rubles a month.

But then the team disbands, a year or two after it is formed. . . . In the director's opinion the reason is that people "fill their pockets," save enough money to buy a car, and, "having no other needs," go back to less intensive, less responsible work that pays 200–250 rubles a month. They do not see the need to work with maximum efficiency.

How different this situation is from the one that existed in the countryside in the postwar years! The leading category of personnel in the branch—agricultural equipment operators—today do not feel any particular need for an extra ruble, much less an extra kopeck.

This fact is by no means of local significance only. It is well known to management and markedly influences the work of enterprises. The interests of production frequently require special, emergency, unscheduled work that is not part of the direct duties of enterprise personnel. It

"Ekonomicheskoe povedenie i ekonomicheskoe razvitie," *Ekonomika i organizatsiia promyshlennogo proizvodstva*, 1980, No. 3, pp. 15–33. Russian text © 1980 by "Nauka" Publishers, the publishing house of the Academy of Sciences of the USSR. Translation © 1981 by M. E. Sharpe, Inc. Translated by arrangement with VAAP, the USSR Copyright Agency. Translated by Arlo Schultz.

would seem that the work is sufficiently well paid and that willing workers would be found to do it. However, many workers are not seriously interested in earning extra money, and the levers of material incentive are frequently powerless.

Does this mean that we have satisfied everyone's needs and that the further growth of production is unnecessary? No, it does not. Even though the present living standard of the Soviet people is incomparably higher than it was, we cannot speak of any kind of "oversaturation" of the requirements of the bulk of the people. What, then, is the matter?

The reason that the rapid growth of production and a further rise in the level of consumption of the working people bump into obstacles in the form of supposedly insufficiently developed mass needs is, of course, not that the cultural level of the Soviet people is low or that they are underdeveloped as consumers. The reason is the poverty of available goods and services capable of creating a sufficiently broad spectrum of powerful "temptations" for the customer. The population's personal savings in banks represent more than half of the annual turnover of state and cooperative trade. This means that even the visible part of cash accumulations would make it possible for people to preserve their customary level of consumption without working for half a year. This argument is, of course, distorted, but it does show how the imbalance in the market situation "undermines" planned management of the development of the national economy.

It is no accident that trends impeding the solution of economic and social problems have recently popped up. Chief among these trends are: the slackening of the growth rate of national income; the lowering of the output-capital ratio; the nonfulfillment of plans for the growth of labor productivity; the shortage of certain important foods and consumer goods in trade, and so on. Here, evidently, the system of "production–supply–consumption" relations has become closed into a circle. It is difficult but extremely necessary to break this circle and transform it into an ascending spiral. Unless this problem is solved, it will hardly be possible to reach high rates of economic development on the road to the intensification of the national economy.

Naturally, the task of coordinating the interests of people and society is not a matter of indifference to Soviet sociologists working at the interface of the economic and social problems of communist construction. The decree of the Central Committee of the CPSU and the USSR Council of Ministers "On Improving Planning and Strengthening the Influence of the Economic Mechanism on Increasing Production Efficiency and Work Quality" requires that scholars devote still more attention to the social, human factor in economic development.

Man and his work

Modern production is more keenly aware than ever before of the significance and complexity of the human factor. Now as never before it senses its dependence on the qualities of the worker, who on the one hand is capable of making highly effective use of the colossal production apparatus that he has created but who on the other hand—by virtue of negligence or low skill level—is capable of working to the serious detriment of the national economy.

The man–machine technological systems born of the scientific and technological revolution make ever greater demands on the education, skill level, and reliability of the work force. In our day the ideal worker at, e.g., a large animal husbandry complex, is more than a graduate of even a vocational technical school, i.e., is a graduate of an animal husbandry technicum. And this is understandable: many people's performance depends on the know-how of such a worker, on his ability to maintain a herd with the help of a system of machinery and equipment.

Not only the work of the individual worker but also the performance of many allied collectives depends on whether a worker shows up for work and whether good or bad decisions are made. However, human reliability and responsibility are phenomena of a different order than machine reliability. A great deal depends on the worker's recognition of his involvement in the common cause, on the degree of his subjective "involvement" in the production process, on the level of his identification with the collective and with the content of his job. Hence the need for a stable work force: workers, specialists, and especially enterprise managerial personnel.

The nation's economy has developed a stable cadre of specialists, managers, and production organizers. They are the "yeast," the "leaven" that makes the economy rise. If management is highly qualified, stable, and full of initiative, enterprises will develop in accordance with long-range objectives, and economic practice will be free of unexpected zigzags and will not fall into the trap of expediency. Unless managers and specialists are involved in the life of the enterprises, unless they link their destiny to the fate of the collectives, there can be no discussion of long-range programs for the improvement of production. Instead we find low and slow-growing results of production activity, workers' lack of hope for better working conditions and wages and their indifference to their work, and a high degree of personnel turnover. The circle closes.

I emphasize: the point is not only that today's worker controls complex and costly systems of machinery and equipment, that he determines their effectiveness and their actual integrity through his attitude toward labor. The objective trend of the scientific and technological revolution lies in the gradual liberation of man from the direct servicing of production processes, from routine, uncreative operations. The worker increasingly concentrates on the performance of purely human functions: on making nontrivial decisions, on the search for optimal technological variants, and on the development of new ideas. The worker himself changes in the process: universal secondary education, higher vocational education, the intensification of all forms of communication, and the fact that people are better informed on the multitude of subjects shape an individual who is self-confident and who has a deep need for self-expression and self-affirmation.

Such a person is capable of doing many things, but he cannot, and indeed does not want to, function as even the most sophisticated kind of servomechanism. Therefore a balance between the creative abilities of today's worker and the potential that production bestows on him is vitally important. In the complex, ambiguous process of development of society's productive forces, the disruption of this balance in one direction or another is fraught with serious consequences.

In the national economic system of "nature–technology–man," the key role belongs to man. And if the human factor proves to be less reliable than the machine, the system is forced to plug in its reserves and backup units in order to offset inevitable losses. According to specialists at the Slavgorod plant, which repairs K–700 tractors in the Altai, 80–85% of the breakdowns are the result of the ineptness of operators and mechanics rather than defective design and manufacture. And just one of these giants costs 18,000 rubles; it outproduces the old DT–54 tractor several times over in the performance of heavy agricultural operations. The statistics on job-related accidents signal the disparity between the sophistication of the worker and the rigorous demands of industrial production.

Reference point: social factors of growth

The history of the development of productive forces has known two powerful "drives" that have forced the worker to adapt to the changing demands of production: unemployment and hunger. Socialist society has freed man from these severe reins. Nonetheless, the problem of coordinating the human and technical factors of production objectively exists. Moreover, this problem becomes more acute with the development of technology, with the growth of self-awareness, and as people make greater demands on the environment and on themselves. The motivation for and specific modes of human behavior in social production, the labor process, the framework of distribution relations, and subsequently the sphere of getting income and consumption currently form a kind of "solar plexus," the center of our society's socioeconomic problems. Essentially it is a question of ways of making the human worker more active, mobilizing social factors underlying the growth of production efficiency; hence scholars' attention is riveted on this question.

The system of socioeconomic relations functions successfully only when all its components interact harmoniously. Sociological science has discovered several points that can be influenced to ensure the development of the system in the direction required by society. Specifically, it indicates three types of social factors that significantly influence the efficiency of production from various aspects: the size, quality, and territorial location of the work force; the complex of living conditions; and the system of socioeconomic relations in social production.

Obviously, modern technological systems can function effectively only if production is supplied with the necessary quantity of personnel with the appropriate skill levels, i.e., if personnel are distributed by branch and region corresponding to the distribution of employment positions. However, this condition is frequently violated, which is one reason for the insufficient effectiveness of scientific and technical progress. The inability to fill high-paying jobs, deficiencies in the education and vocational training of personnel using sophisticated equipment, irrational migratory flows of the population, and high manpower turnover are phenomena that grab society's unflagging attention, are investigated by scholars, and are monitored by planning and administrative organizations.

The second group of factors is the standard, mode, and quality of the population's living. While the size, quality, and location of the work force exert a direct impact on production performance, the living conditions complex plays the role of a feedback mechanism: from the results of production to the work force. The more efficient production is, the more net output created, the higher is the workers' consumption fund, and the more rapid is the growth of nonproductive capital and the social infrastructure. And correspondingly, the smaller the migratory outflow of cadres, the more numerous and better qualified the work force, the more favorable is the dynamics of the efficiency of production.

This is one possible variant of the impact of the aforementioned interrelationships. There is also an opposite variant in which inefficiency of production causes low income and the slow development of the social infrastructure. Hence the migration of personnel, the reduction of the size of the work force, the deterioration of the composition of the work force, and the slow growth of production efficiency. Unfortunately, such a variant happens quite frequently. The modification of the population's living conditions is a unique lever in controlling the movement of the work force. Is it sufficient to regulate the efficiency of production? From our point of view this question should be answered in the negative.

The fact of the matter is that radical change in the living conditions complex of the various groups of personnel is required in order to alter the existing irrational directions of labor mobility and redistribution of personnel between various regions, branches, and occupations. It is sufficient to refer to the need to overcome social distinctions between town and country or the need to improve the living conditions of the population of the eastern regions. Since the deterioration of the living conditions of even individual groups of population contradicts socialist principles, the necessary redistribution of goods can be achieved only by improving the living conditions of disadvantaged groups of workers, i.e., at the price of large additional outlays. Where is the necessary money to come from? When the development of production is efficient, society has at its disposal sufficient reserves for transforming distributive relationships. However, during periods of waning production efficiency, these programs encounter great economic difficulty. This is why the improvement of distribution, while important, is by no means the decisive way to increase production efficiency.

Under these conditions more attention is drawn to the third group of social factors underlying increases in the efficiency of production, which is associated with methods of managing the production activity of people, of "involving" them in economic development processes, and coordinating the personal interests of personnel with the interests of labor collectives and society.

A knot of problems

Sociologists draw a distinction between the direct and indirect regulation of human behavior. Let us illustrate the difference on the basis of the regulation of street traffic. Thousands of motor vehicles travel a complex network of streets, thoroughfares, and crossroads to their destination. How can the control center ensure the prompt and safe arrival of all vehicles at their destination without traffic "tieups," without collisions and accidents, without transport flows being shunted from major arteries to impassable roads? Clearly it can be done in various ways.

The first method requires that the control center have information on the movement of each vehicle, that it regularly update this information, that it analyze and plot an optimal trajectory for the next part of the route (taking the general flow of traffic into account), that it convey to the driver (e.g., by radio) the speed that is to be maintained, where to turn, when to yield, when to pass, etc. Given the slow movement of a few vehicles, such a method would probably be acceptable. However, with the increase in transport flow, the control functions in such an approach would become impracticable.

The other method involves the development of general traffic rules that the drivers themselves must observe. This leaves the control center free to concentrate on monitoring observance of the rules and analyzing their effectiveness and their further improvement. The drivers' status also changes: while in the first instance they primarily follow someone else's bidding, in the latter instance they make their own evaluation of road situations and of routes within the framework permitted by traffic rules, and they select optimum routes. Their labor becomes more creative, and their occupational knowledge, skills, and volitional qualities are mobilized. And what is the general result of the system's operation? In which instance can we expect higher speed, greater safety, and the prompt attainment of the objective? Obviously in the latter instance, in which optimal decisions are sought not only by a single "control center" but by thousands of minds that are well informed about a specific, rapidly changing situation.

The economic system combines two methods of controlling the activity of personnel and collectives. They are centralized planning and the administrative management of production, on the one hand, and the indirect regulation of production activity by means of a collection of rules that predetermine the conditions of economic and social interaction of personnel, labor collectives, and the state, on the other. Plan targets on output, the development of new products, the economical use of supplies, etc., are obligatory and must be met without fail. The area of independent search for an optimal decision is limited here, since the primary function of personnel and collectives is to achieve these targets.

The economic mechanism plays a different kind of a role in the regulation of production activity. The prices on individual types of products, tax rates, the level of payments for capital, norms governing material expenditures, deductions from profits, and basic wage scales act as "red and green lights" indicating the types of economic behavior that are stimulated and approved by the state, the types of behavior that are permissible, and the types that are prohibited and punishable. Every production collective must resolve two related problems: fulfilling the compulsory plan and attaining the best economic results using the full range of possibilities offered by the economic mechanism.

The fundamental significance of centralized planning in socialist economic development is understandable. Its role is analogous to the determination of traffic objectives, to filling out the itinerary that is handed to the driver before he sets out on his run. At the same time, we should like to emphasize the no lesser role that is played by proper economic "signaling." We can easily imagine what would happen if the regulator mixed up the street traffic signals. Wide streets would be empty while alleys and cul de sacs were filled to overflowing with vehicles. . . . One might ask whether something similar does not occasionally happen in the economy. Do the elements of the economic mechanism always stimulate modes of human work behavior that are necessary and advantageous to society?

Unfortunately, not always. Numerous examples of disagreement between local and national economic interests are cited in the press almost daily. Let us take the example of profitability norms in product prices. It would seem that the profitability of producing a product would increase in proportion to its scarcity and the urgency of society's need for it. The scarcest agricultural products today are meat and milk. However, the production of meat and milk is relatively unprofitable for most enterprises and totally unprofitable for a considerable percentage of these enterprises. The additional production of these products is made the responsibility of enterprises by centralized planning, on the one hand, while on the other hand, this additional production is not rewarded, since an increase in the deliveries of meat and milk reduces the enterprises' profits at the same time that it increases their losses.

Difficulties in the specialization of production can serve as another example of the disagreement between economic signals and society's real interests. The national economy is interested in a development of the division of labor that opens the door to more sophisticated technologies and higher product quality. Ministries, agencies, and associations do take certain measures to specialize enterprises; but on the whole this specialization is slow in coming, as if it were encountering a certain degree of resistance. Is the reason the shortsightedness of enterprise management that does not understand the advantages of specialization? Of course not. The fact of the matter is that as a result of differences in the profitability of the production of various products, increased emphasis on specialization is somewhat reminiscent of the story about the cunning peasant and the simple-minded bear who divided up the turnip and cabbage they had jointly grown. Some enterprises are assigned profitable types of products, and the economic results of their activity rise irrespective of the actual quality of their performance. On the other hand, those enterprises that are assigned the turnip "tops" (an unprofitable product mix) are guilty though blameless. Obviously such a system of economic relations does little to further the development of the division of labor. The revision of the wholesale price system slated for the beginning of the Eleventh Five-Year Plan, which is designed to equalize branch profitability in the specialization of production, is all the more timely.

Who does not know, for example, that it is frequently unprofitable for enterprises to produce high-quality products while the production of low-quality products gives them fairly good economic indicators? The pay for complex, creative labor is frequently lower than the pay for simple labor, while a manager's pay is frequently lower than the pay of his subordinates. And what is the price of the fact that enterprises find it more difficult to get rid of superfluous workers than to continue to pay them wages and essentially receive nothing in return! These seemingly unrelated facts are an indication that the system of economic "signals" does not produce the proper degree of agreement between the interests of the individual, the collective, and society, but in a number of instances stimulates behavior that is contradictory to society's interests.

In order to balance the situation and to assure the development of the economy, it is necessary to resort to the techniques of administrative management: to establish plans for the production of each individual type of product in physical indicators, to fund its distribution, to order the distribution of functions among various enterprises, etc. It is possible to replace the economic mechanism by administrative regulation within certain limits, just as it is possible to raise water by means of a system of pumps. But it is complex, costly, and not very efficient. It is more natural and simpler to allow water to flow with gravity, to irrigate the fields in the process, and to use pumps only when no other solution is possible.

As a result of the imperfect state of the system of economic "signals," the channels of economic administrative management become overloaded. The center has to take upon itself the solution of too broad a spectrum of questions, often without sufficient but necessary information. Hence the inevitable blunders, the underassessment of local features, the different kinds of imbalances, and ultimately, the incomplete utilization of reserves and the slower development of the economy.

This is why we received the complex of measures to improve the system of economic levers and stimuli outlined in the July (1979) decree of the party and the government with such satisfaction.

What kind of worker are we training?

Each of us, upon first entering the sphere of social production, runs into the existing system of economic relations. In his labor activity the worker must on the one hand be subordinate to orders and must perform plan assignments, and on the other hand he must heed the signals of the economic mechanism and find in the "economic labyrinth" the mode of activity that will lead to the best result. Upon entering the system of economic relations and becoming subordinate to its action, the worker gradually acquires new personality traits, assimilates certain modes of behavior, and forms a specific social type. The mass worker type, which presupposes a certain attitude toward labor, motivation, and behavior norms in production, in turn becomes an important condition in the functioning and development of the economy.

The socialist principle of distribution according to one's labor—a principle intended to make everyone more active in every way for the good of society—was formulated in severe terms during the first years of Soviet power: "He who does not work, neither shall he eat." Its present meaning is softer: "The more you give society, the more you receive in return." But does the truly large contributor always receive more? Unfortunately, not always. The shortcomings of the rigid administrative regulation of wages, which does not take local production features into account, prompt many managers to find their own solutions and to set an acceptable wage level for the required workers by hook or by crook. And what tricks we find here! Workers who are due for a raise are transferred to a new position entailing the same duties; wages are increased at the expense of the bonus fund; work norms are sometimes reduced to the extent that people can receive pay for two or even three positions, and so on. The result is that some workers come to believe that even though wage regulations must be obeyed, they can be easily circumvented. At the same time, this violates the universal conviction that wages are in all cases truly earned. Some workers become inclined to get the most they can for the least work, to "fish in muddied waters," as the saying goes. And some of them pull it off.

Naturally the foregoing does not apply to all workers. But does the prosperity of a few slackers and idlers influence the views and behavior of other people who see it? They are for the most part young people whose personality has not yet been firmly molded, whose convictions are still in the formative stage. The requirements, interests, and principles of workers whose views are influenced by disharmonious socioeconomic "signals" must not diverge from society's general principles—such is the sense of the decisions of the party and the government on the improvement of labor and wage systems.

Recall the failure with setting up teams operating without work orders. People with a high skill level and the ability to do excellent work did not want to work with maximum intensity and preferred the "quiet life." The system of economic incentives was powerless to awaken their creative potential and left them indifferent to the tasks of the economy and the requirements of society.

We note that according to sociological surveys, wages are by no means the primary reason for turnover and migration, job dissatisfaction, and various forms of labor behavior. The hasty conclusion is drawn that people work not so much to secure the means of subsistence as for the reason that work has become their first vital necessity.

Is it proper to contrast these reasons? Socialist production workers, like everyone else, are material beings whose vital needs are of a material nature. However, the system of socialist production relations is such that labor in social production has become the principal source of people's means of subsistence. Naturally, under normal working conditions people have a material interest in their labor and cherish a job that gives them a decent wage. When they change jobs, they are not indifferent to the material benefits offered by the new job. If this were not the case, there would be cause for alarm. This would mean that the basic system of material stimuli was not doing its job and that people were obtaining a considerable percentage of their means of subsistence from some kind of secondary sources and not from their work in social production.

Let us take another example. A young manager takes an economic risk in order to accelerate the growth of production. Even before the results of the experiment are known, a storm descends on the enthusiast. He is reprimanded, he is "declined and conjugated" as a negative example. Time produces good results, and the experimenter's experience will be extended to other enterprises. Evidently he should be inspired and attempt new reforms. But no, he has changed. Instead of the enthusiast we find a quite cautious official who has "learned from experience." He does not intend to make any more mistakes, "he has had enough," and he will "leave the experimenting to others." He is even-tempered, obedient. He does not make plans. It is easier to control his behavior. Is society not the better for this? Is this the kind of manager we need?

There is yet another channel through which socioeconomic relations influence the formation of a certain type of worker: the absence of punishment for inferior work, for negligent operation of equipment, for absenteeism and tardiness, and for other violations of labor discipline. Many regions of the nation and branches of the national economy are experiencing a manpower shortage. Job vacancies, low shift coefficients, and bottlenecks in integrated technological lines force enterprises to accept the job histories of workers at face value and to keep them at any price. The leadership shames an inferior worker, "berates" a brigade meeting, social organizations, etc. But it rarely goes as far as actual punishment (initially of a financial sort, and ultimately, dismissal). However, careless workers quite soon become accustomed to admonitions. The fact that absentees and bad workmen go unpunished not only reinforces their chosen behavior but also influences conscientious workers who resent being placed in the same category with idlers.

Economic "independence" and its results

The fact that the system of economic relations shapes the worker reflects only one aspect of the question that interests us. The other point is that people, with their requirements, interests, goals, and the means of attaining them, exert a significant reverse influence on the development of economic relations proper. Man is not a cog who can be inserted into a machine and made to work. He does not simply adapt himself to the system of economic relations. He also actively studies the system, finds its weak points if necessary, and tries to exploit them whenever possible. Violations of the norms of economic behavior, which have been noted in party decisions on improving the economic mechanism and in numerous articles in the central press, are an illustrative example. For the sake of brevity I call the totality of these violations of plan, financial, and other norms a "shadow economy" and will subsequently use this purely arbitrary term.

The insufficient reliability of funded deliveries and in some cases the insufficient backing of plan targets with allocated supplies force economic managers to search for unregulated, sometimes illegal ways to obtain needed resources, hire personnel, etc. This frequently is the case, for example, in construction performed by the so-called in-house method, whereby enterprises use their own manpower to build new or rebuild existing productive and nonproductive facilities in accordance with the state plan.

In the agriculture of Western Siberia, approximately 80% of the construction and installation work is performed by the in-house method, for which the plan does not centrally allocate resources. Hence four-fifths of the construction materials and equipment used are not delivered through the plan. Where do they come from? Fuel for machinery comes from Kazakhstan, metal comes from Novosibirsk, coal comes from Kemerovo Oblast, cement from . . . There is evidently a commercial mystery here. There must be payment in meat, honey, the output of fur farms, because the documents do not account for everything. It can be assumed that a considerable part of the turnover of agricultural enterprises passes through these channels. And this is true not only of agricultural enterprises: "I'll scratch your back . . ." relations are developing between industrial, construction, and transport organizations and encompass more and more new spheres of influence.

The result of the development of the "shadow" economy is that some socialist enterprises include in "natural exchange" not only their own output but also acquired means of production. Of this number separate distinction is made for resources that begin to lay claim to the role of a "general equivalent"—livestock, cement, bricks, pipe.

We know that the "shadow" economy is production's reaction to the shortcomings of the basic, planned economy, that both systems of economic relations are as closely interconnected as a real object and its shadow. The "shadow" economy cannot be ignored: the results of its hidden functioning reduce the effectiveness of the planned regulation of production, distribution, and consumption. There is a hidden redistribution of income between social groups that sometimes works to the considerable detriment of public interests.

It is evident that such phenomena should be halted through all possible measures—economic, legal, social—available to society. However, the point is much more complex. First, society does not have the chance to completely halt all undesirable forms of economic "independence," if only because it is not sufficiently informed regarding what is going on. Second and more important, the "shadow" economy has become rooted in the system of basic economic relations and has merged with it. Therefore attention should be concentrated not so much on the fight against individual instances of the "shadow" economy, even though this is essential, as on the improvement of the basic system of economic relations—the methods of centralized planning and the economic mechanism. These key questions were the subject of the July 1979 decree of the Central Committee of the CPSU and the USSR Council of Ministers "On Improving Planning and Strengthening the Influence of the Economic Mechanism on Increasing Production Efficiency and Work Quality." The central idea of the decree is the need for a significant improvement in the system of economic signals and stimuli, limitation of the number of administratively established plan indicators, and the focusing of attention on the social aspects of the development of production and on the mobilization of social reserves.

Sociology's new tasks

The present conditions of society's development confront sociology with new tasks. It must turn decisively in the direction of economics and must study the patterns underlying the productive behavior of people, particularly its dependence on society's system of economic and social relations and on methods of "tuning" the economic mechanism. On the one hand, the time is ripe for the closest "interfacing" of sociological research and economic research, while on the other hand, it is necessary to differentiate their spheres of influence. Economics studies economic relations primarily from the "subjectless" point of view. It views social production and commodity and capital markets as arenas of interaction of a multitude of economic agents, each of which individually does not attract the attention of researchers.

Sociologists study groups of people with a certain economic and social status, with a certain structure of requirements and value orientations that differ by virtue of the nature of their behavior. These people are not only workers employed in social production but are at the same time members of families, owners of personal property, pupils, patients, shoppers, and so on. Sociologists are interested in the ways in which individual groups of workers "enter" production and the ways in which they "leave" it. It is important for them to have a deep understanding of the modes and motivations of human economic behavior and thus to learn how to predict people's reactions to the modernization of economic relations.

Unfortunately our sociology has not as yet organized sufficiently close and comprehensive contacts with economic science. It is possibly for this very reason that in sociological research, the descriptive approach frequently predominates over the managerial approach. Sociologists, while giving a broad and thorough picture of the events in a given area of study (e.g., the qualitative makeup or mobility of the work force), do not always study in sufficient depth the influence of these factors on the effectiveness of production, the probable magnitude of expenditures, and the effect resulting from implementing any measures. Thus far sociologists have more frequently "demanded" sums for the solution of social problems than indicated sources for the growth of production effectiveness due to social factors and the increased activity of the worker.

It is especially important for sociologists to participate in the elaboration of effective means of adjusting the economic mechanism. It is not enough to say that this mechanism does not now meet requirements for the development of production. It is important to determine what it should be like and the kind of social consequences that various changes in its structure will produce. Of course, in actual fact it is impossible to test in practice all conceivable combinations of centralized and decentralized methods of economic management, material and moral incentives, or the system of *ex ante* and *ex post* indicators one after another! The study of socioeconomic processes makes it possible to develop theories on possible variants of economic relations, progressive directions for their development, or the probable results of society's movement along one or another path.

The July (1979) decree of the Central Committee of the CPSU and the USSR Council of Ministers legitimizes the principle that the elaboration of the state plan of economic and social development must be preceded by the collective work of scholars directed toward the search for the most effective avenues of society's future development. The construction of a system of alternate forecasts reflecting the probable results of various modes of management of society is an important part of this work. The aggregate of these forecasts characterizes the extent of society's possible future situation. The performance of this work is inconceivable without the close collaboration of economists and sociologists. What is more, the latter must evaluate social reserves that can be put into operation through the restructuring of the economic mechanism and improvement of the planning system.

The decree of the Central Committee of the CPSU and the USSR Council of Ministers also assigns sociologists the task of finding optimal ways to restructure economic relations and make the transition from the existing system of relations to a new system. The point is that the system of economic relations has an important social component: it is responsible for features underlying the social structure of society, for the array of classes and social strata, and for the content of their relations. Let us take a detail like the degree of centralization of the management of the economy, i.e., the distribution of economic decision-making competence among the primary work collective, the enterprise, the association, and the ministry. A certain degree of centralization of management means a corresponding distribution of rights and duties among various groups of people. It concretizes and defines their real attitude toward state-owned or cooperatively owned means of production and hence their place in the social organization of production and social status.

Accordingly, any, and all the more so a major, restructuring of the economic mechanism infringes on the interests not only of enterprises and agencies but also of social strata and groups. The social economy and the country's entire economy gain from the restructuring of the system of economic levers and stimuli. The population as a whole also gains, since production begins to develop more rapidly, and hence the living standard also grows at a rapid rate. However, some social groups may also lose; moreover, it is not an easy matter to foresee the entire spectrum of consequences of any variant in improving the economic mechanism. Understandably, those social groups whose interests essentially coincide with the direction of projected changes will be the reliable support of the party and government in the restructuring of existing economic relations, while those whose interests are threatened may more or less actively impede the innovations. In order to implement any reforms successfully, it is important to have a clear picture of the structure of social interests and to regulate the behavior of the various groups accordingly. This will promote the solution of the tasks posed by the party.

2 | The Subject of Economic Sociology

In our social development we have now come to a historical watershed, when profound qualititative changes in the forces of production and, accordingly, an improvement in the relations of production have not only been placed on the order of the day, but have also become inevitable. . . . Changes in people's consciousness, in all those forms of social life that we are accustomed to calling the superstructure, should also occur in close interrelationship with this.

Materials of the Plenum of the CPSU Central Committee,
June 14–15, 1983 [in Russian] (Moscow, 1983), p. 9.

Definition of the problem

Economic sociology is a scientific discipline that studies the laws of economic life and the economic development of society using the methods and categories of sociology. The historical roots of this discipline are extremely deep, given the close relationship between the economic and social aspects of society. Attempts to interpret economic development from the standpoint of the social relations reflected in it are to be found in pre-Marxist science as well, although the final methodology of this approach was developed by the classics of Marxism-Leninism. We might mention some of the methodological principles of analysis of the capitalist economy used by Marx and Engels, principles that reflect an

This article was coauthored by Rozalina V. Ryvkina.

"O predmete ekonomicheskoi sotsiologii," *Izvestiia Sibirskogo otdeleniia Akademii nauk SSSR, seriia ekonomiki i prikladnoi sotsiologii*, 1984, no. 1. Russian text © 1984 by the Siberian Section of the Academy of Sciences of the USSR. Translation © 1987 by M. E. Sharpe, Inc. Translated by arrangement with VAAP, the USSR Copyright Agency. Translated by Michel Vale.

orientation toward clarifying the essence of the social relations between the classes and groups entering into them.

The first principle involves the examination of the laws of economic development from the standpoint of the interests, activity, and relations of classes occupying different (including opposing) positions in the system of production, distribution, exchange, and consumption of the social product. According to Marxist theory, the class struggle between the proletariat and the bourgeoisie, which is based on an opposition of class interests with regard to property relations in the means of production, and accordingly, political power, is the pivot of the social mechanism of development of a capitalist economy.[1]

The second principle applied in the social approach of Marxism to an analysis of the economy focuses on the study of the specific position of social classes, strata, and groups. Marx and Engels provided an exhaustive description of the socioeconomic position of the working class and its various strata. Numerous works by the founders of Marxism demonstrate the relationship of this class to the ownership of the means of production, its place in the political system of capitalist society, the level and sources of its income, and its housing and social conditions.[2] This comprehensive analysis of the position of the proletariat was the basis on which the classics of Marxism drew the conclusion that capitalism confronted the working class with the necessity of taking state power in order to reorganize the system of social relations. The same approach was applied by Lenin in his book *The Development of Capitalism in Russia* to study the process of stratification of the peasantry. After a careful analysis of the specific positions of the different strata of the peasantry, Lenin came to the conclusion that within this class a capitalist stratum and a proletarian stratum were taking shape and that, consequently, Russia had already entered the path of capitalist development despite assertions of the Populists to the contrary.

The third methodological principle of the Marxist approach to an analysis of the economy involves the idea that the political factor in economic development, i.e., the role that the state plays in it, should be taken into account. Marx and Engels thoroughly explored the role of the bourgeois state in regulating the position of the working class and the conditions under which its labor was utilized. They also analyzed theoretically the role of the proletarian state in the development of the communist mode of production, and the formation of a new system of production relations.[3] Lenin's study *State and Revolution* is a brilliant continuation and further development of these ideas.

These methodological principles of analyzing the economy were used widely by Lenin in his writings summing up the initial experiences of building socialism.[4] Thus, for example, in examining the question of the most appropriate methods for moving from petty commodity production in agriculture to cooperative enterprises under the specific conditions of Russia in the 1920s, Lenin started out from social relations and social factors. For this reason he was not in favor of "total" socialization of the means of production, or the accelerated recruitment of peasants into cooperative production. As we know, Lenin enjoined the party to exercise extreme caution on this question, to take into account the characteristics of the dual position of the peasantry as both toiler and property owner at the same time, to penetrate into its social psychology, and to put to the practical test and approval those forms of socialization of production that were compatible with keeping some means of production under private ownership in the very first stages.

From what we have said it is clear that an analysis of economic phenomena and processes that views them as the result of the activity of social groups occupying different positions in society and having different interests is a characteristic feature of Marxism. But the growing specialization of the various disciplines in the social sciences, which is not always compensated by their later convergence, has had an effect on the development of modern Marxist social science. In particular, sociology began to develop once again in the USSR in the early 1960s after a long interruption, and its key concern was the study of the social structure of society and its elements, i.e., classes, strata, and groups, as well as the relations binding them together. The development of an empirical sociology made it possible to raise the study of the social structure of society to a new qualitative level, but at the same time it also became divorced somewhat from the study of economic relations.

Of course sociology studies a broad range of phenomena having to do with the economy. Some examples include the attitude of workers to work, their participation in management, the migration and turnover of cadres, choice of occupation, social problems of education, etc. Scientific disciplines such as the sociology of labor, industrial sociology, organizational sociology, etc., study these and similar phenomena. Working together with the corresponding disciplines in economics, these disciplines have made a substantial contribution to improving social relations under socialism.

However, not one of these sciences has set itself the goal of analyzing the development of the economy as a social process reflecting the specific behavior and interaction of classes, strata, and groups in Soviet society. But the need for such an analysis is very perceptible, and is associated with the generally recognized growth of the role of the "human factor" in the development of production, the extremely strong dependence of the economic development of society on social factors, and of the social position of classes and groups on the effectiveness of the economy. In his speech to the Plenum of the Central Committee of the CPSU on June 15, 1983, Iu. V. Andropov said:

> At the Twenty-sixth Congress we emphatically declared the necessity of securing a close relationship between economic policy and social policy. And this is understandable: indeed the ultimate goal of our efforts in the economic sphere is to improve the living conditions of people. We must study and develop our plans, and take into thorough account, and reflect in these plans, the most important factors in the development of society—social, national, and demographic. This should be the unified policy of the party, the unified strategy of social development.[5]

It seems to us that the development of such a strategy requires an especially intensive development of studies at the "borders" between the various social sciences, and especially between economics and sociology. Today this is a need of society, a "social demand" imposed on science, of which scholars are becoming increasingly acutely aware.

There has been a growing interest in our country in recent years in a coordinated study of economic and social problems. Here are only a few of the most interesting examples. In 1982 E. Z. Maiminas published his article "On the Formation of Economic Mechanisms" in which an economic approach was combined with an analysis of the social characteristics of the social system, and in particular its "socioeconomic genotype."[6] According to the author, this genotype is a particular social mechanism based on a specific system of relations of production and management, and the bearers of that system are the social groups that make up the particular society. The contribution of these groups to the development of production depends on their interests, goals, value orientations, and cultural-historical traditions. Attempts have been made to work out the problem of socialist ownership of the means of production taking into account the concrete relations of possession, and disposition over and use of them by social groups. The synthesis of economic, social, and legal approaches is characteristic of the interesting studies by B. P. Kurashvili.[7]

There has also been a parallel movement among sociologists toward some timely problems of economics. Thus a team of Leningrad sociologists led by V. A. Iadov, which studied the process of transformation of work into a prime necessity of life in the 1960s, is now analyzing questions having to do with attitudes toward work and work discipline, and the poor quality of labor. Moscow sociologists have published the results of a study of the economic conditions of ''social justice'' with proposals of ways to improve distributive relations.[8]

Joint studies of the economic and social aspects of societal development are being actively pursued in other socialist countries as well, especially in Hungary. There some very interesting studies are being conducted on the influence of social structure and social relations on the economic development of society.[9] An organic synthesis of an economic and a sociological analysis of processes of economic development has been achieved in the profound and original study by Academician Janos Kornai entitled *Economics of Shortage*.[10] Hungarian sociologists are also actively studying the new economic structures that have emerged in the course of the economic reform, their pluses and minuses, and the possibilities of their further development. Major attention is being devoted in particular to the study of the social aspects of the development of the nonsocialized sector of production.[11] Hungarian economists and sociologists attach especially great importance to the concrete study of the categories of personal and group interests. They are endeavoring to overcome the dogmatic view that the simple fact of establishing social ownership of the means of production guarantees that economic interests of all social groups will coincide, and that group interests will be subordinate to social interests.

As we can see, the problems of economic sociology are quite timely. But the birth of this new discipline has not yet been fully acknowledged by Soviet science. The range of problems that must be dealt with has not yet been identified, the concepts and categories reflecting the essence of this new current have not been developed, much less given currency, and it has not yet developed its own special method. This is quite natural: the shaping of new scientific disciplines requires time.

It is not the authors' purpose here to answer all these questions. Their aim is only to pose these questions, to provide an initial if extremely provisional solution to them, and thereby to attract the attention of the public to the importance of developing this new discipline. What should economic sociology study, or what is its subject matter?

The subject matter of economic sociology

The specific subject matter of this discipline is the laws of interaction of the economic and social spheres of the life of society, of economic and social processes.[12] Here we study the economic preconditions for the realization of the interests of social groups on the one hand, and the social factors and conditions of economic development on the other.

Both these groups of questions are to some extent studied in the borderline disciplines. Thus political economy studies the class structure of society, social differences between the city and countryside, between mental and physical labor, etc. Sociology in turn studies the economic foundations of many social processes—urbanization, migration of the population, the turnover of cadres, etc.

The distinctive characteristic of economic sociology is that its subject matter is not so much the sequences of interrelated economic and social phenomena as the mechanism effecting the link between economic and social development. The task of this scientific discipline is to ascertain the specific ways and means whereby the social structure of society influences the development of the economy, and whereby the economy influences social relations.

Two areas of science are most closely related to economic sociology: the study of the economic foundations of social differentiation of social groups, and the analysis of the social factors affecting economic development. The first area up to now has been studied more thoroughly than the second, and the results of these efforts have been presented in many solid monographs.[13]

The social factors underlying the effectiveness of the economy have also not escaped the attention of scholars, but works devoted to them usually deal with education and training of workers, their living conditions (housing, wages, social amenities, leisure time), and the migration and turnover of cadres. However, the central and most significant factor, the economic behavior of classes and groups occupying key positions in the system of production relations, has so far barely been studied.

But everything that takes place in the economy, from the compilation of production plans to the consumption of output, depends, if not to a critical degree, at least very substantially, on the behavior of the corresponding groups of workers, buyers, and consumers. For example, the behavior of people in the process of forming and developing the family: e.g., the marriage rate and divorce rate, the age at which men and women marry, and intrafamilial regulation of the birth rate, all influence the numerical size, age composition, and location of labor resources. The distribution of the workforce between the city and the countryside, among different regions, and among different branches of the economy is to a considerable extent determined by the directions in which people migrate, and by their shifts from certain branches of the economy to other branches. The occupational and skill composition of workers depends on the behavior of youth in the educational system, the quality of products depends on workers' attitudes toward their work, etc. This means that to pinpoint the influence of social factors on the development of the economy the economic behavior of people must be studied.

But behavior is not an independent factor in the development of the economy. It, in turn, depends on a number of deeper-lying factors the most important of which are, first, the place, the socioeconomic position of social groups, and secondly the external conditions under which this behavior is played out in the economic sphere.

According to the Marxist tradition, the position of classes and groups in socialist society can be described by three basic characteristics: relationship to the means of production, role in the social organization of labor, and their methods for obtaining—and the size of—the consumed portion of the social wealth at their disposal.[14] In empirical sociological studies each of these characteristics is made operational with the help of specific attributes reflecting the nature and content of labor, participation in management, control over the means of production, level of family incomes, etc. The substance of most of these attributes is closely related, so that there are firm grounds for speaking about the integral nature of the socioeconomic position of groups. The distinctive features of this position predetermine group interests, which, in turn guide the behavior of groups. In this context it is relevant to recall the following postulate of Marxism: "The economic relations of any given society are manifested first and foremost as *interests*."[15]

If the direction and the specific modes of behavior of groups are determined by their interests, the margin of freedom they have in their behavior is set by conditions that are external to the groups. The principal regulator of the economic behavior of groups is the economic mechanism, which includes the methods of organizing, planning, and the rewarding of production.[16] The economic mechanism constitutes an integral system of norms of behavior, sanctions, and incentives, the function of which is to guide the activity of work collectives, occupational groups and other groups of workers in the direction required by society. But socioeconomic behavior is regulated not only by the economic mechanism. Legal norms stipulating specific punishments for different forms of antisocial behavior, and modes of behavior imposed upon citizens as a duty and conforming to the interests of society also play an important role here.

However, no matter how minutely activity is administratively regulated, social groups are always left a certain range of freedom in the choice of modes of behavior to realize their interests. Moreover, groups do not always understand and accept the limitations imposed on their behavior by administrative bodies. In those cases where these limitations contradict their vital interests or established traditions and norms, social groups often seek ways to get around a prohibition. In response to this, controlling bodies usually adopt new measures to curtail undesirable modes of behavior, and then groups react in specific ways to these measures, etc. As a result, the socioeconomic behavior of groups and the activity of controlling bodies become mutually attuned, so to speak, and are transformed into a singular kind of dialog.

Social groups interact with one another. Where their interests coincide they combine for joint achievement of their goals, but when their interests diverge a potential for conflict is created. Some conflicts are resolved without the intervention of the state through the independent search by groups for compromise modes of behavior. But if this is not successful, and the conflict of group interests assumes an acute form, controlling bodies serve as arbiters.

In addition to direct contacts, social groups enter into indirect interaction with one another, interaction mediated by relations with the state. For example, nonfulfillment of the plan for grain sales by one agricultural region results in an increase in the target for other regions; the preferential satisfaction of the needs of some farms for tractors and combines reduces the chances of other farms to obtain this machinery. Hence an indirect interaction among groups is accompanied by the same struggle of interests as a direct interaction.

The socioeconomic behavior of social groups is played out not only in the sphere of developing the forces of production, but also in the sphere of improving the relations of production. Indeed, the system of management of the social economy is not something given once and for all. It is shaped, developed, or, on the contrary, unjustifiably conserved for a long time by certain groups of managerial personnel. These groups, as all others, occupy a certain position in society and have their own interests which do not always completely coincide with the interests of society. As K. U. Chernenko observed in his report to the June 1983 Plenum of the Central Committee of the CPSU, "a struggle between the new and the old is going on in Soviet society, as in any body social, and not only constructive but also negative tendencies are operative. Examples are narrow localism and departmentalism, bureaucratism and conservatism."[17]

Since a correspondence between the relations of production and the state of the productive forces is one of the most important conditions for the successful growth of the economy, it is natural to expect sociology to study the mechanisms whereby this is achieved. But in fact no such investigations have ever been carried out. As a result, Soviet science found itself burdened by an oversimplified notion to the effect that under socialism the relations of production were drawn up to the level of the forces of production, without any contradictions between social groups,[18] which of course does not correspond to reality. To fill this gap in scientific knowledge about our society is one of the tasks of economic sociology.

As we have seen, the interaction between the economic and social subsystems of society, each of which has a developed structure, is a quite complex matter. The term "mechanism" is useful for designating the mode of this interaction insofar as it reflects the integrity, the complexity of the structure, and the functional nature of the phenomenon being studied.

By the social mechanism of the development of the economy we mean the stable system of economic behavior of social groups, and the interaction of these groups with one another and with the state with regard to the production, distribution, and consumption of material goods and services, a system that is regulated by historically evolved social institutions, the economic mechanism, and the ongoing activity of the bodies managing and controlling the economy. The function of the social mechanism is to secure an internal unity between the economic and social aspects of the development of society by transmitting "impulses of development" from the social sphere to the economic sphere and vice versa. The specific form in which it functions is the behavior of social groups, while its driving force is their interests.

How are the social mechanism of the development of the economy and the economic mechanism of management control correlated? We regard the economic mechanism of management control of the economy as constituting a most important part of the social mechanism of its development, since it plays a key role in regulating the economic behavior of groups. The economic mechanism for managing the economy serves as a "skeleton" for the social mechanism, but it is not the whole of the latter since it comprises neither the social structure of society, nor the behavior and interaction of its groups. While the economic mechanism for managing the economy (in the sense we give to it here) is to a considerable extent the result of the purposeful activity of managing bodies, the social mechanism of the development of the economy as a whole is a natural-historical phenomenon formed, as it were, behind the back of society. It therefore has more inertia and is much less manageable than the economic mechanism.

Historically specific variants of the social mechanism of a socialist economy may of course vary in quality, i.e., they can be more or less effective. One may evaluate their effectiveness on the basis of results of the economic and social development of society. The former are characterized by the level of effectiveness, and the growth rates of production, while the latter are characterized by changes in the social structure of society and in the social qualities of people.

As Karl Marx observed, man is the "imprint" of the social relations of which he is a part. Hence every specific system of relations of production creates a special social type of man corresponding to its quality. The characteristic features of this man are determined by firmly internalized norms of behavior, transformed into personal traits, in the sphere of production, distribution, exchange, and consumption. The social type of the subject of economic activity inherent in any society is characterized by the prevalence—and the level at which they are manifested—of such qualities as love of work, reliability, conscientiousness, an enterprising spirit, honesty, ability to take independent decisions or calculated risks, collectivism, and on the other hand by such features as indifference to the work at hand, individualism, money-grubbing, lack of principle, irresponsibility, etc.

The social types of workers can be assessed only by evaluating their predominant modes of behavior. But the concepts of "type of behavior" and "type of worker" do not coincide. The difference is that behavior is more fluctuating: its manifestation not only depends on the type of worker, but can also change as external conditions change, while the membership of workers in a specific social type is a long-term factor. The influence of this factor on the development of the economy is felt not only throughout the work life of a particular generation, but also after that generation leaves the scene, insofar as the personality traits and norms of behavior of older generations are transmitted to the younger ones. In particular, this explains the historical continuity in the characteristics of ethnic groups of workers (e.g., Russian, Estonian, Georgian), reflecting the specific features of the path of historical development traversed by these respective peoples.

The social type of worker predominating at a particular moment is in part the result of existing social relations, but it also bears some imprint from previously existing conditions. Hence it has considerably more inertia and is not easy to modify. However, the inertia of a social type of worker and its resistance to regulation heightens the significance of the influence exerted on it by the social mechanism of development of the economy. Although this influence is not able to modify an existing type of worker in the necessary direction within a short period, it nonetheless is a long-term and ultimately achievable goal.

Thus we have described the social mechanism of development of an economy, which should, we think, be the principal subject matter of economic sociology. Now let us go on to describe its method.

The method of economic sociology

The specific features of the subject matter of economic sociology are reflected in the distinctive features of its method. If by method we mean a way of effecting the "movement" from the real state of an object being studied into the language of scientific concepts, then the method of economic sociology can be described by answering two questions: (a) what system of concepts does this science use; (b) how does it use these concepts to obtain the required knowledge of the structure of the object being studied and of the laws of its development.

The specificity of the scientific concepts and categories with which economic sociology must operate derives from the principal goal of this science, namely, to coordinate and synthesize the economic and social development of society. To achieve this goal a suitable scientific language is necessary. In the particular case this language will be based on categories worked out in sociology, while the sphere to which they will be applied will be the economic life of society. The use of sociological categories equips the investigator with that specific "prism" which makes possible a social approach to the economy.

The specific results of the development of the problems of economic sociology, and the richness of the ideas it comes up with will depend first on the thoroughness with which the sociological concepts and categories are used, second, on the accuracy of the content given to them, and third, on the extent of their practical use, i.e., on which particular aspects of the economy will be subjected to sociological analysis, and how deeply this analysis will be conducted. We do not have the opportunity in this article to describe the concrete ''technology'' of applying sociological categories to analyze economic processes. Hence let us limit ourselves for the time being to merely an initial systematization of the necessary categories.

The scientific concepts and categories used by economic sociology can be divided into two groups according to their origin: those that are specific to the particular science, and those that it has in common with several other sciences. The concepts and categories of the first group can in turn be subdivided into three types.

The first type consists of concepts that specify the types of socioeconomic groups and the attributes of their position in society. Among the groups whose behavior mediates the relationship between the economic and social development of society, economic sociology considers first, collectives of formal organizations (enterprises, institutions) and their primary subdivisions; second, occupational, official, income, and consumer groups; and third, territorial (urban, regional) groups. Each type of group is characterized by both general attributes (level of income) and specific attributes of position, proper to it alone. For example, the position of territorial groups in the population is characterized by the natural and climatic conditions of the corresponding regions, the extent to which the surrounding territory has been developed and settled, and the types and sizes of settlements (village, small or large city). In contrast to this, the position of groups of white-collar officials is characterized by the range and balance of their rights and duties and their place in the organizational structure of management, while the position of occupational groups is characterized by the content and conditions of their work, the level of their salaries, etc.

The second type of concept pinpoints the content of interests, and the types and modes of behavior of socioeconomic groups. Since the category of interests has not yet been sufficiently developed, the system of concepts concretizing it is relatively narrow. Interests are divided into individual, group, and social in accordance with the extent of their generality; into economic, political, and intellectual with regard to their orientation; and into progressive, reactionary, and conservative with regard to the objective tendency of their social development.[19] In addition, we may distinguish between latent interests and interests of which the subjects are aware, along with those taking shape and those having found external expression in the corresponding behavior of groups.

The types of socioeconomic behavior are familial, occupational and job, educational and vocational, migratory and mobile, commercial, organizational and managerial, and certain others. Modes of behavior are differentiated with regard to their types. For example, the migratory and mobile behavior of groups is characterized by the frequency with which they change their place of residence or job. The groups of stable workers, constituting the basic nucleus of collectives, and the "flitters," who never stay anywhere for long, are distinguished with regard to this criterion. Other types of socioeconomic behavior are similarly characterized by other modes of realization.

The third type consists of concepts and categories that reflect the link between social and economic processes. The categories of the social mechanism of development of the economy, and concepts describing its elements and internal relations, occupy a central place among them. Space does not allow us to go in detail into the content of these concepts, many of which are being introduced by us for the first time. One example would be the concept of the special mechanism of socioeconomic reproduction, regarded as an element of the general mechanism of development of the economy.

The above-described concepts and categories reflect the main content of economic sociology and distinguish it from its allied sciences.

But the language of economic sociology is more than just the concepts specific to it. In addition to these, it includes categories that are, first, common to all areas of sociology, and second, to all or most social sciences. For example the category of "social structure" is used in sociology, in history, in political economy, and in philosophy. The same applies to such scientific categories as social class, stratum, group, collective, city, countryside, region, enterprise, social organization, social relations, etc. Many categories are borrowed by economic sociology from the language of political economy (for example, relations of production, ownership, economic planning, cost-accounting, material incentives, living standard, incomes, personal consumption, and many others).

While economic sociology is mainly distinguished from allied sociological disciplines by its subject matter, its method is what distinguishes it from allied economic disciplines. As we have shown, economic sociology focuses on the behavior of specific socioeconomic groups in the sphere of social reproduction. Purely economic phenom- ena and processes (e.g., the profitability of production, the increase in capital investments, etc.) are regarded on the one hand as external conditions determining group behavior, and on the other as the result of behavior. This approach is not at all a typical, or at least a principal approach in other economic disciplines.

Economic sociology also has a special approach to the concept of social relations, so central to the social sciences. In most sciences this concept is used to designate not the concrete interactions of groups occupying different positions in society, but links mediated by relations of people to material goods (property in the means of production, the relationship between prices of different groups of commodities, etc.). In contrast, economic sociology studies the concrete interactions of social groups: workers and managers of enterprises, city dwellers and rural inhabitants, representatives of various work collectives, etc.

The economic and sociological approaches to the study of economic development complement rather than contradict one another, as may be demonstrated in the study of socialist property. The economic sciences study this problem mainly from the standpoint of the macrorelations of possession and control over the means of production as set down in legislation and economic policy. The behavior and interaction of groups in respect to the utilization of social property, as well as their subjective relationship to it, is not studied in economics. In contrast, sociologists study the concrete relation of specific groups to social and personal property. When this relationship deteriorates, they determine its causes, and devise the conditions in which workers must be placed in order to improve their relation to social property, and to work in social production.

Areas of development of economic sociology

In evaluating the main areas of development of economic sociology, we must first begin with the specific features of the subject matter and method of the science, and then go on to the demands of practice. Soviet society requires the scientific elaboration of a system of manage- ment of production that would ensure the increased effectiveness of social labor, help to improve socioeconomic processes, heighten inter- est in work, and improve the social type of worker. Unfortunately, neither economists nor sociologists have as yet completed such a proj- ect. One of the reasons for this is that Soviet social science has hitherto devoted little attention to the study of the economic behavior of groups and the social factors operative in it. But a system of management of the economy geared to the effective use of the "human factor" can only be developed on the basis of a thorough linking of economic and sociological investigations.

In what areas must the problems of economic sociology be developed? It seems useful to distinguish five such areas.

1. The study of the composition and qualitative characteristics of those social groups whose interaction constitutes the basis of the social mechanism of economic development. We must determine what these groups are (distinguish their basic types), evaluate their qualitative composition and quantitative content, their dynamics, the content of the functions they perform, and the social forms of their interaction in the economic sphere.

2. The study of the objective laws, norms, and modes of economic behavior of social groups, including the maintaining of private subsidiary and household plots, as well as episodic forms of employment. In this sphere, all types of behavior having an essential influence on the economy must be studied.

3. An analysis of the conditions on which the economic behavior of groups depends. This is first, the socioeconomic position of groups: the possibility of utilizing the social means of production, participating in the management of the economy, the structure of sources of income, the level and forms of income. Second, this includes the management of the economic activity of groups by state bodies: the level of production plans, their balance with regard to resources, price levels, the organization of sale of output, wage rates, the content of official instructions, the norms of legislation, etc.

4. The study of the socioeconomic consciousness of social groups, in particular, their interests, needs, values, opinions, life plans, ideas about ways to improve social relations, etc. A study of these characteristics of consciousness is necessary to evaluate the qualities of workers and construct a social typology of them.

5. The development of a system of socioeconomic management of the economy that will ensure the integration of the interests of different groups with one another and with the state; working out concrete ways to effectively utilize labor and industrial potential, and the experimental testing of these means in actual practice.

The development of these areas would enable economic sociologists, together with representatives of other sciences (economists, specialists in law, specialists in management) to participate in working out and adopting an effective social mechanism for economic development, the core of which would be, in our view, the economic mechanism with extensive feedback channels.

The above areas reflect the general logic of research into the problems of economic sociology; from a description of particular groups to a study of interactions between them and the state, and then the social mechanism of development of the economy as a whole; from an analysis of what is taking place today to the development of improved forms of socioeconomic relations, their experimental testing, and their practical implementation.

To pursue this logic, it is useful to break down the main object of study, namely, the social mechanism of the development of the economy, into a series of "projections" each with a simpler structure. These are, in particular:

1. A territorial "projection" that proposes to study the socioeconomic position, interests, behavior, and interaction of regional and community groups, and their role in the economic development of society.

2. An organizational-production "projection" that studies departmental, administrative, and organizational factors in the behavior of work collectives, the social aspects of interaction of departments, enterprises, and primary subdivisions, as well as the influence of these interactions on economic development.

3. A social-managerial "projection" that studies the position, interests, behavior, and interactions of vertically hierarchized groups of workers in social production.

4. A personal economic "projection" that studies the position and behavior of different groups in the private sector of production.

5. A consumption and income "projection" that studies groups differing with regard to the level and source of income, their behavior in the sphere of distributive relations, and accordingly in production.

We regard these "projections" as relatively independent subsystems of the social mechanism of the development of the economy, although in their aggregate they should quite thoroughly reflect its internal structure. The above set of five "projections" is clearly not complete. It reflects only those aspects of the social mechanism of the development of the economy, whose structure is clearest and which can be practically studied at the present level of our knowledge.

Economic sociology has deep roots in the history of social thought, but it is also a timely scientific discipline addressing the tasks of improving developed socialism in the USSR. Iu. V. Andropov observed at the June 1983 Plenum of the Central Committee of the CPSU: "In developing our economic plans, we must learn to comprehensively take into account and reflect in them the most important factors in the development of society—social, national, and demographic. This must be the unified party policy, the unified strategy of social development."[20] We hope that the working out of the problems of economic sociology will facilitate the accomplishment of this extremely complicated task and enable us to take into account the social factors of economic development more extensively and more thoroughly than has been done heretofore.

Notes

1. K. Marx and F. Engels, "Manifest Kommunisticheskoi partii," *Soch.*, 2nd ed., vol. 4; Marx, *Kapital*, vol. 1, chs. 5, 8, 11, and 17; *ibid.*, vol. 2.
2. Marx, "Polozhenie fabrichnykh rabochikh," Marx and Engels, *Soch.*, vol. 23; Engels, "Polozhenie rabochego klassa v Anglii," *ibid.*, vol. 2; *idem*, "K zhilishchnomu voprosu," *ibid.*, vol. 19, etc.
3. Marx, "Kritika Gotskoi programmy," Marx and Engels, *Soch.*, vol. 19; *idem*, "Grazhdanskaia voina vo Frantsii," *ibid.*, vol. 21; Engels, *Anti-Diuring*, section 3, ch. 4. *Gosudarstvo, sem'ia, vospitanie, ibid.*, vol. 20.
4. V. I. Lenin, "O kooperatsii," *Poln. sobr. soch.*, 5th ed., vol. 45; *idem*, "Veliki pochin," *ibid.*, vol. 39.
5. *Pravda*, June 16, 1983.
6. *Ekonomika i matematicheskie metody*, 1982, vol. 18, no. 3.
7. B. P. Kurashvili, "Gosudarstvennoe upravlenie narodnym khoziaistvom: perspektivy razvitiia," *Gosudarstvo i pravo*, 1982, no. 6; *idem*, "Sud'by otraslevogo upravleniia," *EKO*, 1983, no. 10.
8. *Sotsial'naia spravedlivost' i puti ee realizatsii v sotsial'noi politike*, edited by V. Z. Rogovin et al. (Moscow: ISI AN SSSR, 1982).
9. "Formirovanie sotsialisticheskoi obshchnosty liudei. Problemy ravenstva pri sotsializme," *Problemy mira i sotsializma*, 1980, no. 10.
10. R. G. Karagedov, "Mekhanizm funksionirovaniia sotsialisticheskoi ekonomiki," *Izvestiia SO Akad. Nauk SSSR*, 1982, no. 11, ser. obshchestv. nauk no. 3.
11. Istvan Gabor and Petr Galasi, "Vtorostepennaia ekonomika. Nekotorye ekonomiko-sotsiologicheskie problemy chastnoi sferi pri sotsializme," *Sotsiologiia*, 1978, no. 3.
12. By economy we mean the subsystem of society responsible for production, distribution, exchange, and consumption of material goods and services necessary for maintaining and reproducing human life. The distinctive characteristic of economic relations consists in their property or possession aspects.

The social sphere of society is the sphere of relations between groups of people occupying different positions in society, participating to different degrees in its economic, political, and intellectual life and differing not only in the level but also in the sources of their income, the structure of personal consumption, lifestyle, level of personal development, and type of social consciousness.

13. See for example *Sotsial'naia struktura sovetskogo obshchestva*, edited by V. I. Semenova, vols. 1 & 2 (Moscow, 1980); M. N. Rutkevich, *Sotsial'naia struktura razvitogo sotsialisticheskogo obshchestva v SSSR* (Moscow, 1976).

14. Lenin, "Velikii pochin," p. 15.

15. Engels, "K zhilishchnomu voprosu," vol. 18, p. 271.

16. The scientific literature contains various conceptions of the category of economic mechanism. By economic mechanism we mean the system of economic and administrative control of the development and functioning of the economy.

17. K. U. Chernenko, "Aktual'nye voprosy ideologicheskoi massovo-politicheskoi raboty partii," *Pravda*, June 15, 1983.

18. *Filosofskii slovar'*, edited by I. T. Frolov, 4th ed. (Moscow, 1981), p. 116.

19. *Filosofskii entsiklopedicheskii slovar'* (Moscow, 1983), p. 214.

20. *Materialy Plenuma Tsentral'nogo Komiteta KPSS 14–15 iiunia 1983 g.* (Moscow: Politizdat, 1983), p. 13.

3 | Economics Through the Prism of Sociology

The intensive specialization of modern science has made the simultaneous investigation of complex natural and social phenomena by various fields of knowledge commonplace. No one today is surprised when physicists analyze chemical, geographers analyze demographic, and sociologists analyze economic processes. After all, every science views the same phenomenon from its own point of view and makes its own specific contribution to the general knowledge concerning it. Interdisciplinary research of complex phenomena provides a more complete, multidimensional picture of an object.

Economic sociology, which employs sociological techniques to investigate patterns of economic development, is a new discipline that is developing at the interface of social sciences. It differs from allied disciplines studying the same phenomena by virtue of itsw specific view of economic life as the interaction of social groups that, in V. I. Lenin's words, occupy a different place in the historically determined mode of production, perform specific production-related and social functions, are vested with dissimilar rights and obligations, and pursue special interests. The economic sphere of social life then takes on the appearance of a "theater" whose many "actors" as members of labor collectives more or less successfully play the role of producers, organizers of production, distributors of material resources, planners, sup-

"Ekonomika skovz' prizmu sotsiologii," *EKO*, 1985, no. 7, pp. 3–22. Russian text © 1985 by "Nauka" Publishers, the publishing house of the USSR Academy of Sciences, and *Ekonomika i organizatsiia promyshlennogo proizvodstva*. Translation © 1986 by M. E. Sharpe, Inc. Translated by arrangement with VAAP, the USSR Copyright Agency. Translated by Arlo Schultz.

pliers, accounting clerks, inspectors and workers in the service sphere and, as family members, play the role of personal household plot owners, householders, shoppers for food and manufactured goods, consumers, etc.

The activity and interaction of groups that play an economic role are subject to a scenario written by society. For example, working conditions and employment are regulated by labor legislation, the terms of purchase and sale of products—by state prices, and the interaction of allied enterprises—by economic contracts and the allocation of stocks according to plan.

At the same time, the economic life of society depends to a significant degree on the actions and decisions of people in accordance with their personality traits and group and individual interests. It is specifically on this socially determined subjective contribution of participants in economic activity that sociologists are concentrating their attention. How do people behave in the economic sphere? What are the macroeconomic consequences of their behavior? Why do people behave in one way and not another? Can behavior be controlled? What means can be employed to make behavior regulated by personal and group interests most effective to society? It is the job of economic sociology, which is only now taking its first steps, to answer these questions.[1]

Behavior and social processes

Group and individual behavior influences all aspects of economic activity and to a considerable degree predetermines its results. Let us take as an example human behavior that influences the formation, distribution, and utilization of labor resources. The point of departure is the natural reproduction of the population in the course of which people are born, mature, and die. The more the birth rate exceeds the death rate, the more rapid is the growth of population and society's labor resources. The birth rate depends on the age at which men and women marry, on the stability and length of marriages, and on the prevailing view of the optimal size of the family. The dynamics of the birth rate affects the growth of labor resources with a lag of 15–20 years. Their feeble growth in the 1980s is the direct consequence of the decline of the birth rate between 1965 and 1970. As we see, even such types of behavior that at first glance appear to be a private family matter become a factor of economic development upon becoming integrated into social and demographic processes.

Considerable influence on the dynamics of population and labor resources is also exerted by the death rate, the level of which depends to a greater degree than commonly thought on the behavior of social groups. A healthy, dynamic life style, a rational work and rest routine, observing safety procedures, and the timely prevention and proper treatment of diseases help people to live and work longer. The opposite type of behavior, particularly the abuse of alcohol and hypodynamia, frequently results in grave illness and premature death.

One of the basic needs of the economy is to improve the quality of labor power and in particular, the educational and skill level of the work force. The state is improving the network of schools and is developing production-technical training schools, technicums, and institutions of higher learning. However, the final result of this activity depends primarily on students' attitudes toward their studies: after all, the assimilation of knowledge is by its very nature voluntary; it is virtually impossible to command academic excellence. Therefore, the real knowledge that is acquired by students for whom learning is an internal need and by those for whom learning is an external necessity is far from the same. And that is not all. Even though from a legal standpoint, secondary education in our country is mandatory, in actuality, some of our young people who are not disposed toward learning do not go beyond the eighth grade, or else merely go through the motions of completing school for the sake of the diploma. Naturally, knowledge acquired in this way is superficial and does not seriously influence the effectiveness of future labor activity.

Upon graduating from school, young people who are guided by personal interests decide whether, and if so, where to continue their studies or else where to start work. The many decisions that are made in this regard—decisions that are outwardly independent of one another—when implemented in practice, form the social process that ultimately predetermines the dynamics of the vocational-skill structure of society's work force.

Finally, let us take the territorial distribution of labor resources. As we know, a little more than 10 percent of the nation's population lives in Siberia and the Far East; the same area accounts for 15 percent of the nation's productive fixed capital and between 50 and 90 percent of its fresh-water reserves, timber, fuel-energy resources, and mineral raw materials. The shortage of labor power is the principal constraint on the rate of development of the eastern regions. In the European part of the nation, on the contrary, the population is comparatively large, but natural resources are far less plentiful. Consequently, population migration from west to east is in society's interest. In actuality, however, as noted at the Twenty-sixth CPSU Congress, people "still frequently prefer to migrate from north to south and from east to west even though the rational distribution of the productive forces requires that the migration be in the opposite directions."[2]

Migration is a form of socioeconomic behavior. Before making the decision to move to a new place of residence, a family weighs all the pros and cons because, according to the saying, "moving twice is the same as going bankrupt once." Families usually decide to migrate only if they are certain that everything will be better for them in the new place, even though everyone has his own interpretation of what is "better." Some want to go where the climate is milder, where the cost of living is lower, where working conditions are healthier; others like the combination of intensive labor and high earnings; still others are attracted to places that have a predominantly youthful population, that offer interesting leisure pursuits, that provide opportunities to form families earlier. When it selects a new place of residence, each group is guided by a special interest and its own hopes. But the aggregate of individual moves forms mass migratory flows between republics and regions, between town and country, and promotes the territorial redistribution of population and labor resources in various directions.

The vocational-labor behavior of workers in the workplace predetermines the quality of social labor, which in turn influences the effectiveness of production, the quality of output, and the rate of scientific-technical progress. Production and economic activity in the personal sector of the economy (personal household plots, collective gardens, individual construction, etc.) affects the level and structure of national income and the correlation of incomes of social groups. Purchasing behavior divides products of labor into use values that have won public recognition and products that are rejected by consumers as worthless. Here, too, macroeconomic processes become the integral sum of a multitude of independent behavioral acts.

From the foregoing, it obviously follows that the study of the socioeconomic behavior of people and the clarification of its patterns are capable of shedding additional light on the processes of economic development and of explaining certain trends observed here.

The main force behind behavior: interest

But what, strictly speaking, is behavior? How does it correlate with the more general concept that reflects the active attitude of people toward the surrounding world, with reality?

The basic content of human activity is the transformation of nature's material into a product that satisfies certain needs. Economic activity is expressed in the production, shipment, storage, and sale of material goods and services, in the planning and organization of production, in the formation of the economic mechanism, in the organization of credit and monetary circulation, in the distribution of resources, income, etc.

Behavior is the subjective aspect of activity, i.e., the aggregate of actions that reflect people's internal attitude toward the conditions, content, and results of activity. Behavior is always regulated by a more or less conscious goal and presupposes a certain freedom of choice of actions from a set of possibilities. The more strictly the content and conditions of activity are regulated, the narrower is the area of manifestation of behavioral factors and the lesser is their influence on its result.

The choice of mass forms of economic behavior is based on interests that are defined in the literature as "the real causes of social actions that are behind the direct causes—motives, intentions, ideas—of the social groups and classes participating in these actions."[3] Interests form at the borderline between the objective conditions of vital activity and group consciousness. As an element of consciousness, they at the same time directly reflect the particulars of the objective status of groups. A unique feature of socialist society is the communality of the basic interests of classes and groups that consist in the reinforcement of the guiding role of the Party, in the development of socialist social relationships, in the preservation of peace, in the realization of national security, in the conservation of the natural environment, and in raising the level of the material and social well-being of the people. But in addition to common interests, social groups also pursue their own interests, which they occasionally try to realize even when they are contrary to the interests of other groups.

There is no end to examples of non-coincidence and struggle of economic interests. Let us recall only a few common situations. The producing plant is interested in fulfilling and overfulfilling the "gross output" plan and in lowering production costs, even at the expense of the deterioration of product quality to a certain degree, whereas the customer is primarily interested in product quality. A construction organization strives to deliver an incomplete project on schedule at any price and pledges to correct defects later; the future users of the contruction project, however, insist on its completion exactly according to plan. The book trade is interested in rapid turnover and in printings that are sold out in 2–3 days; authors and book buyers, on the other hand, would like to see published books on the counter for quite a long time. Dwellers in a small settlement find it convenient if a bus stop is very close to their home. But low ridership makes the stop unprofitable and the bus route is discontinued. While the number of examples could be multiplied, it is obvious from the given examples that the interaction of groups pursuing different interests is at the very basis of society's economic life.

The June (1983) Plenum of the CPSU Central Committee noted that in Soviet society "as in any other social organism, there is a struggle between the new and the old, and both creative and negative tendencies are operative. Examples are localism and departmentalism, red tape and conservatism. The reasons for these and other similar phenomena should be revealed, and ways of eliminating them should be found."[4] The phenomena named at the June Plenum of the CPSU Central Committee are nothing other than abnormal forms of the manifestation of the interests of certain groups of managerial personnel that contradict the interests of society as a whole. Behind the majority of social contradictions, there is usually a clash of interests of various social groups.

What determines interests?

The interests of social groups depend on their status in the system of economic, social, and political relationships. In *The Great Beginning*, V. I. Lenin provided the classical definition of social classes as large groups of people who differ in their place in a historically concrete mode of social production. He proposed that these groups be described on the basis of three major interconnected features, specifically: (a) their role in the social organization of production; (b) their relationship to the means of production; and (c) methods of obtaining and the size of the share of social wealth that they have at their disposal. It seems that these features are entirely applicable for the differentiation of not only classes but also more restricted groups that differ in their social status—intraclass, interclass, and nonclass (which, by the way, is what is done in Soviet sociology).

Then, on the basis of the first feature, groups are differentiated according to the character of their functions in society and the specific content of their labor. Among them: workers in social production, representatives of political power, servicemen, writers, artists, etc. Production personnel are differentiated on the basis of this feature into departmental-branch groups and labor collectives of enterprises and organizations on the one hand and, on the other, representatives of physical and mental, subordinate and managerial labor, and certain types of occupations.

The second of Lenin's features divides groups with dissimilar rights and powers vis-à-vis the ownership, possession, disposition, and use of the means of production. Workers in the state and collective farm-cooperative sectors of production as well as owners of personal means of production not employed in the social sector (owners of personal household plots, small craftsmen, etc.) are primarily differentiated from this point of view. There is further differentiation of groups that differ in the breadth and content of the right to dispose of social property. Such, for example, are aides who distribute production resources and finished products among branches, enterprises, and territorial units; material-technical supply, wholesale and retail trade workers; and economic managers at one level or another.

The social significance of the use of the means of production is twofold. Its first meaning is associated with the quantity, quality, and technical improvement of the means of production used by occupational groups and labor collectives. Thus, metallurgical workers use costly, sophisticated equipment in the work process, which presupposes high skills and responsibility. Auxiliary workers, on the other hand, use simple hand tools. The result is substantial differentiation in both the material rewards and social prestige of these groups. The necessity and ability to use sophisticated, one-of-a-kind technical devices in the work process raise social status of the corresponding groups of workers.

The second meaning of the feature is associated with the possibility of the semilegal use of social means of production (and sometimes part of the final product as well) for personal needs or for sale on the side. Three groups of workers can be differentiated from this point of view. The first consists of people engaged in labor, the content and conditions of which exclude the possibility of using social property for personal ends. The second group consists of workers who have the possibility of using the means of production entrusted to them to satisfy their own needs or to extract income. The reference is to truck drivers, train conductors, rural machinery operators, and workers in certain other categories. The third group is made up of workers who by virtue of their situation have the possibility of maneuvering certain production resources (feed, construction materials, etc.) or part of the final product.

Groups of families with different income sources and levels are differentiated on the basis of the third feature cited by Lenin. The principal sources of income in socialist society are: wages from social production, cash payments from social consumption funds (to students, invalids, pensioners, single mothers, etc.), the output of personal labor, and material aid from other persons (alimony, inheritances, etc). Most working people who for the most part live on the basis of income derived from social production are divided into groups of low-, average-, and high-income families. In addition to them, society also has groups whose principal source of income is large-scale private plots that produce a highly marketable surplus. There are also people, albeit few in number, operating in the so-called "shadow" economy who use unlawful means of producing income.

At first glance, the social groups that are differentiated on the basis of each of the three features are independent of one another. In fact, this is not the case. The affiliation of workers with various branch, territorial, vocational-skill, and official groups (their place in the social organization of labor) usually predetermines their relationship to the means of production, the level of their wages, and the general structure of their income. Thus, socioeconomic status is not a random set of values of several unconnected features, but is a whole characterization of social groups that predetermines their interests and behavior. Consequently, the behavior of groups in the socioeconomic sphere, which at first glance frequently seems random, has quite deep roots in the social structure of society. For the most part, the modes of this behavior have regular patterns. But if this is so, they are the subject of sociological analysis. They should be studied as part of a complex with regard to (1) relationships between various types of behavior; (2) economic and social factors that determine behavior; and (3) the possibility of directing economic behavior into the channel of social interests.

Administrative management of activity or economic regulation of behavior?

Centralized distribution and the regulation of economic activity express the systematic character of the socialist economy, whereas human behavior embodies its spontaneous aspects. The systematic character plays the main and spontaneity a secondary role in the development of the socialist economy. However, from this it does not by any means follow that systematically controlled economic activity and socially determined behavior can and should be contrasted with one another as something "good" and "bad," as "truly socialistic" and "not entirely socialistic." After all, behavior expresses the conscious character of activity, its subjective basis, and its dependence on human social qualities. The nature of these qualities determines the behavior of groups and the influence of behavior on the results of economic activity. Various forms of behavior may raise or lower its results.

The movement for communist labor, the organization of student contruction brigades and youth housing cooperatives, the activity of innovators and inventors, the adoption of higher socialist pledges by labor collectives, the proposal of new forms of socialist competition, the search for effective forms of labor organization and wages, the holding of various kinds of socioeconomic experiments at the local level, etc., can serve as examples of the working people's behavior that fully corresponds to social interests. Behavior that is contradictory to the interests of society is frequently manifested in the low quality of labor, in mismanagement of the means of production, in weak labor and production discipline, in upward distortions, in speculation, theft, etc. The state is naturally interested in the development of positive and the elimination of negative forms of the working people's economic behavior. But how can this be achieved if behavior reflects subjective orientations that are predetermined by personal interests?

There are two basic approaches to the regulation of behavior: (a) the administrative restriction of the freedom of choice of its forms through the detailed regulation of activity; and (b) the indirect economic regulation of the content of behavior through the adjustment of group interests. Both approaches are equally necessary and complement one another. Thus, a planned economy would be entirely impossible without the direct administrative management of the basic types of economic activity. But excessively detailed regulation contradicts the status of the working people as co-owners of the means of production, hinders the development of a "feeling of proprietorship," and impedes the full disclosure and utilization of abilities. It deprives labor of its creative elements and truly human essence and transforms it into a time-serving process.

On the other hand, the weakening of the external regulation and oversight of labor and economic activity leads to the intensification of elements of spontaneity in the development of the socialist economy, to the growth of the role of behavioral factors. A sophisticated and ramified system of economic incentives and sanctions coordinating group interests of workers with social interests becomes necessary. However, it is incomparably more difficult to develop and implement a system of economic management than to manage with the aid of directives and orders.

Consequently, the task is to find the correlation of administrative and economic methods of management of behavior that is rational for various concrete conditions in the economic sphere. This is attained by the appropriate "tuning" of the economic mechanism, i.e., by the choice of such a variant that best corresponds to the state of the productive forces.

The economic mechanisms of socialist countries differ substantially from one another in the correlation of direct (administrative) and indirect (economic) methods of economic management. The role of administrative management is relatively great in the Soviet national economy. Economic activity here is regulated more strictly and in greater detail; the area for the realization of behavior is relatively narrow.

The fact of the matter is that the basic qualitative features of the present mechanism for managing the national economy formed back in the 1930s.[5] While this mechanism has been repeatedly modernized and improved since then, the initially adopted correlation between administrative and economic methods of managing activity and behavior has remained essentially the same. At the same time, the Soviet economy's productive forces have changed beyond recognition over the decades. Technical inputs per workers have increased tens of times, the type of technologies employed has changed dramatically, and the demands that are made upon the skill level and responsibility of workers and on social labor discipline are incomparably higher. There have also been enormous changes in the social characteristics of workers. This was expressed not only in the eradication of illiteracy and the rapid rise of the level of general and specialized education, but also in the higher degree of scientific-technological and sociopolitical awareness of workers, the increasing complexity of their needs and interests, and in the development of their legal and personal consciousness. Change in the subjective qualities of workers in turn led to the increased diversity of economic behavior, to the increased complexity of its content and motivations, to the more intensive and complex interaction of "controlling" and "controlled" groups at all levels of the social hierarchy.

In addition to this, the significant rise of the living standard has reduced the economic need for workers to work intensively for the sake of obtaining the means of subsistence. Most social groups today have the possibility of choosing between intensive work in quest of higher earnings and limited participation in social production for average pay.

On the one hand, major social changes have raised the demands that are made on the flexibility, elasticity, and controllability of the work force, while on the other hand they have made the regulation of the behavior of workers more complex than ever before. The effectiveness of administrative methods for managing economic activity has declined, and indeed the existing economic mechanism as a whole has become insufficiently effective under the new conditions. This is outwardly manifested in frequent disruptions of the systematic character of production and material-technical supply, in the relaxation of economic incentives, in the faint dependence of income of some workers on the results of their labor in social production, etc.

The main social consequence of the lag of the economic mechanism behind the demands of the time may be the growth of the management apparatus accompanied by the decline in the effectiveness of the management of the activity and behavior of workers. The fact of the matter is that the administrative management of activity has internal constraints and under certain conditions may turn into its opposite. Indeed, administrative control is directed first and foremost toward the restriction of behavior that contradicts social interests. But control functions are vested in people who also have their own interests. As the press shows, people who are dutybound to oversee the observance of state interests do not always make the grade and in some cases are capable of sacrificing society's interests for the sake of personal interests. Hence, it is also necessary to oversee their activity and behavior.

This principle leads to a multilevel system of administrative management and oversight that inevitably acquires bureaucratic features. Owing to the disparity between words and actions, between accounts and the actual facts, it becomes more difficult to oversee and control economic processes.

The self-evident conclusion is the need to alter the general strategy for managing the human factor of production: to put contraints on the administrative regulation of economic activity and to concentrate attention on the regulation and stimulation of progressive modes of behavior. This need is recognized by the Party and is reflected in decisions of CPSU congresses and Party plenums. The Party links the urgent task of economic intensification with a more democratic management of the national economy, the development of the initiative of production managers, the renunciation of petty administrative tutelage over their activ-

ity, the increased labor activity of the work force, and the better utilization of society's labor and creative potential. This means giving workers more choice in behavior selection as well as increased rights and
more responsibility for economic performance.

The transition to predominantly economic methods of management
raises many new and complex problems pertaining to the improvement
of the economic mechanism, which have been widely discussed in the
press and on the pages of *EKO*. Since these problems are not within the
purview of the article, we will not dwell on them here. Let us turn
instead to the relationship between the economic mechanism and the
social structure of society.

The economic mechanism and the social structure

The improvement of the economic management mechanism should
simultaneously provide an integrated solution to economic and social
problems. However, it may be that the economic and social effectiveness criteria of this mechanism not only fail to coincide, but may even
contradict one another. Thus, most socialist countries permit the operation of small private retail trade, public catering, or personal service
enterprises. They help to utilize more completely the labor potential of
the population, including the population that is not employed in social
production, and to better satisfy the demand for services. Such a
measure is highly effective from an economic point of view. At the
same time, the emergence of a group of private owners of means of
production who do not participate in social production and who receive
higher incomes violates the principle of distribution according to one's
labor and leads to the increased social differentiation of society.

Such collisions require the conscious discussion of development
alternatives and the establishment of economic and social priorities. If
preference is given to economic goals, there must be special oversight
of the social results of change in the economic management mechanism. But if priority is assigned to social goals, the economic results of
the reform must be carefully monitored. Generally speaking, the social
consequences of change in the economic management mechanism are
no less significant than the economic consequences.

The influence of the economic management mechanism is greatest
on the social structure of society, i.e., the composition and status of its
classes, social strata, and groups. It would appear that proper attention
has not yet been devoted to this relationship. The problem of improving

the economic mechanism is frequently investigated from purely economic positions without regard to its relationship to the social structure; the dynamics of this structure is analyzed independently of change in the economic management mechanism. We refer to two aspects of the same phenomenon because the economic mechanism is a specific form of realization of the economic aspect of production relations, while the social structure of society reflects their social aspect. As is known, the classical scholars of Marxism-Leninism have always viewed the economic and social aspects of production relations in their indissoluble unity, and our science should not lose this valuable tradition.

But how is this relationship realized, and what significance does it have for economic development? We have already discussed the factors that determine the place of social groups in the socialist mode of production. Most factors are of an economic nature and directly reflect the particular features of the existing system of economic management. Accordingly, in a certain sense it can be said that the economic management mechanism determines the social structure of society and the status of social groups.

Indeed, it is difficult to name an element of the economic mechanism, the change of which would not influence the status of one or another group of workers. Let us take, for example, the problem of overcoming departmentalism in the management of the national economy. A substantial reduction in the number of branch ministries and the restriction of their functions in managing the national economy will obviously bring about a dramatic decrease in the size of the state economic management apparatus and will appreciably diminish the influence of certain categories of executives. The development of the economic independence of enterprises will increase the rights, economic influence, and social prestige of enterprise managers, whereas ministry executives will lose some of their rights. The reform of the wage system, change in principles governing the distribution of social wealth, the removal of restrictions on the size of personal household plots—every such step will inevitably cause corresponding changes in the social structure and social differentiation of society.

One conclusion is that the actual development of production relations is not only and not so much the result of the occupational activity of workers specially engaged therein as it is the complex interaction of socioeconomic groups that occupy different levels in social production and that pursue contradictory interests.

The social mechanism underlying the improvement
of production relations

The June (1983) Plenum of the CPSU Central Committee noted that "we have reached such a stage in our social development that profound qualitative change in the productive forces and a corresponding improvement in production relations have not only matured, but have also become inevitable."[6] The resolution of the CPSU Central Committee on the work of the Institute of Economics of the USSR Academy of Sciences confronted social scientists with the task of studying ways of improving socialist production relations in close relationship with ongoing social processes.[7] The question arises as to the kind of social mechanism that ensures improvement in socialism's production relations.

According to the opinion that has been affirmed in our social literature, in socialist society there are not and cannot be groups that are interested in the preservation of obsolete relationships, and hence, there is also no basis for social conflicts in connection with their change. These premises can be interpreted in the sense that the development of socialism's production relations is not so much of a social as a technical nature, so that it is only necessary to note the need to improve them and then to take the necessary measures in good time.

However, the facts do not confirm this point of view. They show that it is not enough merely to understand the reasons for the deceleration of economic growth or even to know possible ways of surmounting existing obstacles in order to bring about the necessary changes in economic practice. While the present stage in the improvement of economic management started in the mid-1970s, the Twenty-sixth CPSU Congress maintained that the work in this direction over a period of many years had been too slow and indeterminate. Thus, attempts to make wiser use of economic methods frequently ended in the return to administrative management methods, and there was no appreciable expansion of the economic rights of enterprises. The cited phenomena are not atypical.

The subjective attitude of social groups toward the projected reform of the economic management mechanism has been more and more intensively studied by economists and sociologists in recent years; the initial research findings have been published. Together with personal observations, this makes it possible to describe briefly the orientation of various groups toward the proposed changes.

Attitudes toward the reform of the economic management mechanism in the direction of the wider use of economic methods of management appear to be most highly differentiated among groups selected depending: (a) on their place in the economic management hierarchy; and (b) on the affiliation of workers with certain social types.

Three major vertical collaterally-subordinated groups are differentiated under (a): workers belonging to (1) organizations responsible for the interdepartmental management of the national economy (the State Planning Committee, the State Committee for Labor and Social Problems, the State Committee for Prices, the Ministry of Finance, and others); (2) branch ministries and departments and their territorial administrations; and (3) associations and enterprises. Differences in the attitudes of these groups toward the projected reform of economic management are to a considerable degree associated with the fact that prestige and social status in the first and third groups rise as a result of the reform, whereas they decline in the second group. The fact of the matter is that the present system of economic management is characterized by the relative debility of both the lower and upper levels of management and by obvious hypertrophy of the intermediate level. In order to give the productive forces more room to grow, we must restore the proper correlation between vertical levels of management while at the same time expanding the rights of both central economic organizations and enterprises.

Two social types of workers with substantially different attitudes toward the projected reform of the economic management mechanism are differentiated under (b). The first type is represented by the better educated, more highly skilled, and energetic segment of cadres who strive for full self-realization in their work and in some cases for professional advancement as well. These people usually feel that under the proper conditions, they could work more intensively and efficiently, receive a correspondingly higher income, and live a better and more interesting life. Most workers of this type strive for a higher degree of independence in professional decision-making, for more room in which to display their initiative so as to work to the full extent of their ability and to consume according to the results of their labor. Workers of this type are evidently represented in different proportions at all hierarchical levels and are the main social force in improving economic relations. The other social type comprises the less skilled and relatively less active segment of cadres. These workers fear, not without foundation, that the new conditions will make their work more difficult, require them to upgrade their skills, to retrain, to change their work style, and will mean the worsening of their situation; they are therefore in no hurry to change the way things stand.

If the effort to improve production relations is to be successful, there must be on the one hand a well-conceived social strategy that is capable of consolidating groups that are actually interested in the intensification of the economy and the corresponding reform of management methods, while on the other, the actions of groups inclined to impede the solution of urgent problems must be blocked. This is precisely how the party formulates the task when it indicates the need for the prompt identification and resolution of mounting contradictions. Therefore, it is especially important, as the Extraordinary February (1984) Plenum of the CPSU Central Committee noted, to secure a close interrelationship between the economic, social, and spiritual progress of developed socialist society. The raising of the economy to a qualitatively new level presupposes the necessary social prerequisites for doing so.

Notes

1. For more detail, see: T. I. Zaslavskaia and R. V. Ryvkina, "O predmete ekonomicheskoi sotsiologii," *Izvestiia SO AN SSSR. Seriia ekonomiki i prikladnoi sotsiologii*, 1984, no. 1, issue 1, pp. 9–20. [For an English translation, see the preceding essay in this volume, "The Subject of Economic Sociology."]

2. *Materialy XXVI s''ezda KPSS*, Moscow, Politizdat, 1981, p. 54.

3. *Filosofskii entsiklopedicheskii slovar'*, Moscow, Sovetskaia entsiklopediia, 1983, pp. 213–214.

4. *Pravda*, June 15, 1983.

5. See, for example: B. P. Kurashvili, "Sud 'ba otraslevogo upravleniia," *EKO*, 1983, no. 10, p. 34; R. G. Karagedov, "O sovershenstvovanii khoziaistvennogo mekhanizma," *Izvestiia SO AN SSSR. Seriia ekonomiki i prikladnoi sotsiologii*, 1984, issue 1, no. 1, p. 22.

6. *Materialy iiun'skogo (1983 g.) Plenuma TsK KPSS*, Moscow, Politizdat, 1983, p. 115.

7. "O povyshenii roli Instituta ekonomiki Akademii nauk SSSR v razrabotke uzlovykh voprosov ekonomicheskoi teorii razvitogo sotsializma. Postanovlenie TsK KPSS," *Pravda*, February 14, 1984.

4 | The Social Mechanism of the Economy

The system of social production or, for short, the economy, may be examined and studied from the most diverse positions. For the technologist, this is a process of gradual transformation of material and energy flows into a finished product. For the cyberneticist it is the movement of management information, a process of adopting and implementing decisions. For the economist it is primarily the production and distribution of the national income and social product. All of these professional pictures of reality implicitly assume the presence of people: it is people who transform raw material into final output, exchange information, create and distribute social values. Thus far, however, these are some kind of average, faceless people, devoid of any human qualities.

But the most urgent problems of the times are rooted in just this "purely human" aspect of the economy. The role of the human factor in the economy grows more critical with the development of scientific and technical progress. Today, a number of categories of workers are employed on automatic tools and assembly lines the cost of which equals the wages they will receive throughout their entire working lives. Engineers take technical decisions each of which involves tens of thousands of rubles gained or lost for the state. Scientists develop or assess projects costing billions and tens of billions of rubles (for example, the projects of diverting some of the northern rivers into the basin

"Sotsial'nyi mekhanizm ekonomiki," *Znanie–sila*, 1985, no. 10, pp. 3–5. Russian text © 1985 by "Znanie–sila," published by the All-Union "Knowledge" Society of the USSR. Translation © 1987 by M. E. Sharpe, Inc. Translated by arrangement with VAAP, the USSR Copyright Agency. Translated by Michel Vale.

of the Caspian Sea, and Siberian rivers into the basin of the Aral Sea). But whether these projects come into existence is decided by the most ordinary people, our contemporaries, who have not only the necessary level of qualifications and a certain breadth of horizon, but also specific interests, who not infrequently want to take one particular decision rather than another.

Social scientists long ago came to the conclusion that the role of man today in production is a decisive and key role and that it will only continue to grow. But man, in contrast to raw materials and machinery, is a social being: he has his own values, inclinations, and interests, which he strives to realize.

Social man, man in an environment with other people, in interactions with his social group and with representatives of other social groups—this is what sociology studies. The economic life of society is one of the objects of study of sociology.

There have been many sociological studies involving the economy: sociologists study the attitudes of workers to their work, their participation in the management of production, the migration and turnover of cadres, the choice of occupations, and the social problems of education. The sociology of labor, industrial sociology, and the sociology of organizations are all closely related to economics, and essentially study the social aspects of economic problems. But when we put together the results of these often very skilled and serious studies, we do not get an integral sociological picture of the economic life of society. What emerges is a mosaic that does not make it possible to reconstruct the social mechanism of the development of the economy, but only brings out certain details and elements of this mechanism.

The concept of the "social mechanism of development of the economy" is almost unknown in the press. It is only in the process of being formed in scientific laboratories, and has been put to the test in the first studies of a new scientific current, namely, economic sociology. Let us try to see how the economy looks from the perspective of this new discipline.

*   *   *

The first thing we see is a multiplicity of social groups that interact with one another in the economic sphere. These groups occupy different positions in society. They have divergent interests and unequal rights and obligations; they are linked by the multiple and varied relations between them. In this gigantic "theater" each has his own role: on the one hand, workers, producers of various products or their distributors, organizers of production, suppliers, accountants or inspectors, plan developers, etc.; on the other hand, there are those who receive the various incomes, buyers, consumers of all possible goods and services, possessors of household plots and private plots, etc.

The interaction of social groups, as indeed all social processes, obeys its own intrinsic laws. But the socialist state must control them in accordance with a plan. What means does it have at its disposal for doing this?

Economic activity is regulated by legal norms and administrative decisions: these are laws, "norms set down in the law," plan targets, economic agreements, job instructions, etc. A certain structure of management organizes the activity of people within the framework of statutes, and the system of economic incentives should give people an interest in operating within this framework as effectively as possible. All this together constitutes the economic mechanism of managing the economy. This is the main "instrument" enabling the state to guide the economic activities of all social groups in the necessary direction.

The traditional notion of how the economy of a socialist society develops may be represented in somewhat oversimplified form in Figure 1. The effectiveness of the economic development of society is dependent on the scale and quality of the work of all its members. Their work in turn is guided by the economic mechanism. When this mechanism begins to lag behind the needs of the expanding forces of production and cause breakdowns, it must be corrected. The more promptly and more skillfully this is done, the more quickly will the difficulties of the new stage be surmounted.

This notion is in part valid. But it presupposes three oversimplifying assumptions.

First, that the economic activity of people is fully amenable to planning and control.

Second, that the development of the socialist economy does not depend on the social structure of society, its division into classes, strata, and groups (and I mean not the simple reference to the existence of classes and groups, but to a "working model" of the social structure that would explain the economic development of society).

And finally, third, that the development of a system of management of a socialist economy itself takes place in accordance with this schema, as if automatically, without a struggle of human interests.

The essential and perhaps even the decisive part of reality is situated

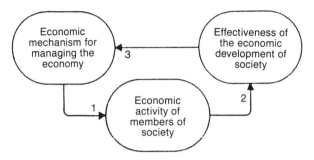

Figure 1.

outside the confines of this paradigm. I mean the economic behavior of people, which is not prescribed by any instructions, which is dictated by group and personal interests, opinions, and preferences, which are by no means only economic. This is essentially the personal contribution of people to economic activity.

Does it influence the effectiveness of economic development of society? And if so how?

* * *

People marry, get divorced, raise one, two, or three children, have varying attitudes toward their health, and observe safety regulations negligently or scrupulously. The ratio between the number of men and women, the relative proportions of people of different ages in the structure of the population of different regions, depends on what we may call demographic behavior, and this is by no means a matter of indifference for the economy. It determines, for example, the size and the nature of the demand for goods and services. The structure of the able-bodied population, the ratio of the number of persons first entering the workforce and those going into retirement, also depends on demographic behavior. The growth in the labor resources of the country was very low in the Eleventh and Twelfth Five-year Plan periods because the birthrate had fallen in the Eighth and Ninth Five-year Plan periods. Among the many reasons for this, by no means the least important was the sharp increase in the number of working women even as the number of nurseries and kindergartens remained inadequate.

Not only the general results of demographic behavior, but the way it shapes up in the different regions of the country is also important for the economy. Today practically the entire increment in the working-age population is accounted for by Central Asia, while in Russia, Belorussia, the Baltic Republics, and the Ukraine its size is declining. Yet it is the economy of these republics that is most in need of workers.

People are also still inclined to move from place to place. The calculations of our Institute of Economics and Organization of Industrial Production of the Siberian Section, Academy of Sciences, USSR, showed that the migration at the beginning of the '80s of one worker from the European part of the country and from Central Asia to Siberia or the Far East would by the year 2000 have caused an average increase of 8,000 rubles in the personal consumption fund of the nation's population. And about a million more workers are still needed in the eastern region. But migration is a voluntary matter and people migrate only if they are sure that living conditions are better in the new place. If their expectations are not borne out they go back. In 1983 only a few more people migrated to the Far East than left there—indeed, they could not be held there by force. The migration flows, which amount to a multitude of individual migrations, are more likely to be from north to south and from east to west, than *vice versa*, as they should be for the growth of the economy.

Let us leave demography. Educated and skilled workers are needed for production, but a person cannot be forced to study what is needed; in the extreme case, he can be kept in school, vocational-technical institute, technicum, or higher education for years, but no more. Indeed even this is not always successful. For example, according to the data of our study, despite the law on universal secondary education a portion of rural youth not only does not have such education but will not go on to get it.

And least of all can the quality of education be ensured by administrative measures.

Too often a diploma in secondary or higher specialized education in any occupation will not guarantee the aggregation of necessary knowledge and skills by the person possessing this education. There are many reasons for this—they could be discussed *ad infinitum*—but one thing is clear: a person cannot be forced to study well, conscientiously, and with interest by decrees and demands.

Teachers seek for ways to attract young people to study, to plant the seeds of and develop a desire for knowledge in them. The school reform of course will help them to do this, but no reform in itself can instantaneously and directly change people's behavior at any age. Yet the quality of future workers—the decisive factor for the economy—is determined in the school, in the technicums, and in higher educational institutions.

People change their jobs and their occupations, and the structure of employment emerges from the totality of these voluntary and varied decisions, while some sectors, industries, and enterprises are faced with an extremely acute labor shortage.

People have different attitudes to their obligations, and the fulfillment of plans and norms and the effectiveness of utilization of labor time will depend on the extent to which they have a sense of involvement in their jobs, their conscientiousness, and other personal qualities.

People refuse to keep a cow on their household plots, or pass summer evenings in their vegetable gardens, and we obtain or go without a certain portion of agricultural output, and the aggregate social labor time fund and the productivity of social labor decrease or increase.

Many people endeavor to increase their family budget by seeking and finding additional sources of income—sometimes fully within the law, and sometimes beyond it. The result is a specific distribution of the efforts of people between the public and private economies, and at times disproportionalities arise in the incomes of different social groups, and a "shadow economy" appears.

It is also quite obvious to what extent the sale of produced goods, and consequently, the normal course of the reproductive process depend on buyers' behavior, and how important our behavior as consumers is for the effectiveness of the economy. It is difficult, for example, to make the purchase of wheat abroad at a rather high price fit in with the grain feeding of cattle or with wastage. Indeed production, exchange, distribution, and the consumption of output are phases in one and the same process.

I do not think that any further proof is necessary that people's behavior influences literally all aspects of the development of the economy. Consequently, we must find a place for it in the model reflecting this development and understand its driving force.

*   *   *

The driving force of behavior is personal and group interest; man consciously shapes his goals on the basis of them.

These interests are largely—and, what is more important, mainly—common interests: a moral and political unity is the characteristic feature of Soviet society. All its members have a vested interest in strengthening Soviet power and in the achievements of socialism, in a stable peace on earth, and in conserving the natural environment.

However, every social group has its own special interests, which may come into contradiction with the interests of other groups.

The consumers of goods and means of production are interested, for example, in high-quality products, and often are willing to pay more for this quality. But the producers sometimes "chase after gross output" to fulfill the plan, and hitherto product quality has been a secondary concern for many. Consumers want a full range of goods permanently in the shops, but for those working in the retail trade a rapid "turnover" of goods, in which these goods simply drop out of circulation, is more important. Those who will live in new houses are interested in a careful and conscientious completion of well-thought-out designs, while builders often try to finish a building as quickly as possible despite many unfinished details.

Party documents have often cited the struggle between the old and the new, the progressive and the conservative, and this struggle goes on in any body social. The harm done to our society by narrowly conceived departmental interests, localism, and bureaucratism has been frequently noted. But these phenomena have a social content: the group interests of various administrative and managerial personnel are manifested in these phenomena in a socially selfish form.

However detailed the administrative regulation of the economic life of society may be, socioeconomic groups always retain some freedom of choice in their behavior, and consequently preserve the possibility of realizing their interests in some way or other, to some degree or other. If the restrictions imposed by decrees and instructions contradict the vital interests of a group or the established traditions and norms, people often find ways to get around the prohibition. Administrative bodies respond by taking new measures to curtail the undesired behavior, and the groups respond to this in a definite way. The socioeconomic behavior of groups and the activity of administrative bodies is an original and permanent dialogue.

Relations between groups are complex and varied. Groups unite when their interests coincide and seek reasonable compromises when their interests are contradictory; they appeal to administrative bodies when the contradiction is too acute and they are not able to find a compromise. They have an influence on the interests and behavior of other groups even when they do not enter into any direct relations with them, but act indirectly: if someone has managed to get for himself additional tractors and combines, this means that someone else will not have enough of such machinery, or if someone has been "overloaded" with the plan for grain sales, this plan will be increased for someone else. The indirect interaction among groups is accompanied by the same struggle of interests as a direct interaction.

But what are these social groups? How are their interests formed, on what do they depend, why are they different for some groups than for others, and indeed even in opposition to one another?

Marxist theory holds that social interests are determined by the position of classes, strata, and groups in the totality of society's economic, social, and political institutions. In a developed socialist society, differences between classes are so unessential that we can say classes have almost completely merged. Indeed, the position of farm workers depends on occupation (tractor driver, milker, agronomist), on place of residence (village near a city or remotely located), on size of their private plot, and is practically independent of whether they work on a collective or a state farm.

In our view the factors determining the position of social groups in society must be sought in their different opportunities for disposing of and utilizing the social means of production (in this respect, the position of a minister differs from the position of a factory director, the position of a tractor driver or truck driver or worker on a livestock farm differs from the position of an accountant, doctor, or teacher); in their varying degrees of participation in the management of the economy and society (undoubtedly, the democratization of the management of production is a characteristic feature of many nascent forms of organization of labor, in particular, the "brigade contract" is changing the social position, the interests, and the lifestyle and thoughts of rank-and-file workers); finally, such factors are to be sought in the structure of the sources, the size, and the forms of income.

The formula "two classes and one stratum" no longer describes the real differentiation in a developed socialist society. But it by no means follows from this that all social differentiation has disappeared.

It has become the custom in economic literature to say that the incomes of Soviet people are formed from three main sources: a) wages; b) pensions, subsidies, and stipends; and c) incomes from personal private plots. This distinction is too rough, for it requires that incomes with differing social content be subsumed in the same category. For example, the term wages includes both fixed salary rates and piecework earnings, as well as author's royalties, and the earnings of freelance construction workers. Or take incomes from private plots:

the plot may be a little garden or it could be a highly productive farm equipped with the latest technology. In expeditions into rural areas in Siberia we encountered families with up to nineteen cows and forty fattening pigs. In some republics, small-scale private crafts are permitted. This is a very specific source of income and it undoubtedly forms a social group with special interests and special economic behavior.

People's behavior is random only at the first, most superficial glance; it has deep roots in the social structure of society. The economic and the social are directly fused in it and it serves as a connecting link between a given moment in the life of society and the preceding historical stages, since the social structure itself is the consequence of a long historical development.

Thus in our model of the development of the economy one more component must be included: "The socioeconomic position and interests of social groups," and an arrow must show the influence of this component on the economic behavior of groups.

*   *   *

Then how is the position of groups in society itself formed?

Clearly that position will depend first and foremost on the overall wealth of society. One cannot consume what has not been produced.

Experience has shown that when the economy grows at a rapid rate the socialist society actively resolves its social problems, raising the material well-being of those who are at the time in a relatively disadvantaged position. Wages are increased in sectors where they are below the average, housing is built at an accelerated pace, and the size of pensions is increased. Briefly put, the labor of social groups increases the wealth of the nation, and this enables society to implement its social program.

The second extremely important factor influencing the position of social groups is the state of the economic mechanism for managing the economy. This mechanism and the social structure of society are essentially two aspects of the same system of relations of production. There is hardly anyone today who would dispute that the economic aspect of these relations is manifested in the economic mechanism. Their social aspect is manifested in the social structure of society. Perhaps this is less obvious but it is nonetheless undoubtedly so. Any essential corrective applied to the economic mechanism changes the relative position of social groups: some gain from it, others lose.

It is natural that people should endeavor to improve their position.

Of course this concerns not only increasing incomes; people also value highly the opportunity for self-fulfillment, initiative, creativity, and the right to participate in decisions that are important for their jobs and their lives. The economic mechanism largely determines the latitudes of such opportunities. It balances rights and duties, and also determines the relationship between incomes and labor contributed. And when the economic mechanism is running smoothly people will satisfy their interests with means that are desirable and effective for the growth of the economy.

Considerable social potential for the further development of the economy lies latent in economic behavior characterized by initiative. The cultural and professional level of a worker in socialist production is today such that an interested and creative attitude on his part toward the job at hand is capable of reaping very rich fruits.

Here are some data from one of our surveys in Altai. Sixteen percent of workers and collective farmers and only 10 percent of managers felt that they could not work better than at present. As regards the conditions under which they could work more effectively, 68 percent of workers and collective farmers and 42 percent of managers mentioned improvement in the organization of production, and approximately 30 percent of each group mentioned improvement in the quality of management and better wages.

The experience of the better agricultural, construction, and industrial enterprises also indicates that the labor potential of workers is by no means thoroughly utilized. The brigade contract in construction, the collective contract on a "family basis," contracts in agriculture, the work system created in the Kaluga turbine factory, all represent experience in shaping new economic relations accumulated at the level of the brigade subunit, the brigade, and the enterprise as a whole. We cannot rest on these experiments, however reassuring the results may have been.

* * *

Thus the social mechanism of the development of the economy in our model has been enriched by the introduction of the concept of "economic behavior" as well as the box "social position and interests of socioeconomic groups" which determines this behavior (Figure 2). The result is three relatively closed circuits. We have already spoken about one, namely, that reflecting the planned management of the economy: the economic mechanism organizes and directs the economic

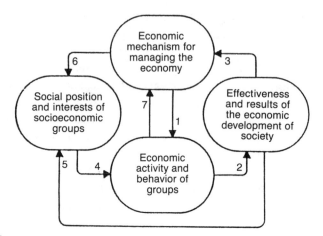

Figure 2.

activity of workers; this activity determines the effectiveness and the results of economic development; if these results do not completely satisfy society, the economic mechanism is readjusted.

A second circuit reflects the influence on the economy of factors not susceptible to direct planned management: a specific social structure of groups with different social positions and different socioeconomic interests is formed under the influence of the economic mechanism. People implement these interests in their economic behavior and that behavior influences the effective development of the economy. This in our view is a first approximation to the social mechanism of the development of the economy.

The third circuit shows the influence of the social structure and of the interests of social groups on the economic mechanism, as mediated by their economic behavior.

This theoretical model provides a fuller conception of the driving forces of the development of the economy, and enables us to understand how the "human factor" acts upon and influences it. Economic sociology, which regards as its subject matter the economic behavior of people, and the interaction of social groups and their interests, must therefore effect a genuine synthesis of economic and sociological studies.

In what directions will it develop as it explores more thoroughly and enriches the theoretical paradigm presented here?

Above all, it still remains to be ascertained what precisely are the socioeconomic groups whose interaction predetermines the development of the economy. What kinds of people are included in them? How large are these groups? Which are diminishing and which are growing in size? What are the functions of each?

After distinguishing the groups themselves, that which is specific and characteristic in their behavior must be found. The objective laws of this behavior must be studied and the principal conditions shaping and directing it must be determined.

Of course we will also be interested in what stands ''behind behavior,'' namely, the characteristics of the consciousness of people in these different social groups: their interests, needs, values, opinions, and life plans.

This research material is necessary to coordinate to a maximum degree in practice the interests of different groups with one another and with the interests of society as a whole, to mark out specific paths for the effective use of the labor potential, and to experimentally verify them in practice.

This great undertaking has only begun. We are confident that it will help us to find a solution to many of the current acute problems of today's economy.

Creative Activity of the Masses
Social Reserves of Growth

**The decisive condition for the acceleration
of social and economic development**

The party's strategy of accelerating the nation's social and economic development is aimed at the qualitative transformation of all aspects of Soviet social life and at converting it to a higher qualitative level of development. This means radical renovation of the material-technical base of social production, substantial improvement of the system of social relations, the progressive transformation of people's living conditions and way of life, and the invigoration of all sociopolitical life. The party associates the realization of these objectives directly with man's heightened creative activity. Socialist society, the CPSU Program states, cannot effectively function without finding new avenues of development for the creative activity of the masses in all spheres of social life. The larger the scale of historic goals, the more important is the proprietary, interested, responsible, conscientious, and active participation of millions [of people] in their attainment.

It is not by chance that there has been a substantial increase in interest in the human factor in social development in recent years. It reflects an objective trend toward a dramatic intensification of the impact of human activity not only on the living conditions of people themselves, but on the state of large ecosystems all over the globe.

"Tvorcheskaia aktivnost' mass: sotsial'nye rezervy rosta," *EKO*, 1986, no. 3, pp. 3–25. Russian text © 1986 by "Nauka" Publishers, the publishing house of the Academy of Sciences of the USSR, and *Ekonomika i organizatsiia promyshlennogo proizvodstva*. Translation © 1987 by M. E. Sharpe, Inc. Translated by arrangement with VAAP, the USSR Copyright Agency. Translated by Arlo Schultz.

After all, the economic, social, and ecological effect of an average hour of work by modern man is equivalent to days, if not weeks, of his parents' and grandparents' labor.

The main reason for this is the rapid increase in technical inputs per worker. We may recall that as recently as the 1930s, wheat was harvested with a sickle or horse-drawn mowing machines, ditches were dug with shovels, earth was hauled away in wheelbarrows, and gold was washed manually with pans. The relatively small losses inflicted by the negligence of individual workers corresponded to the low productivity of manual labor. Today, we see an entirely different picture: grain is harvested by motorized combines; powerful excavators and bulldozers do the work of hundreds of workers; a five-man team services a dredge costing several million rubles. Under the new conditions, a sober, skilled, and reliable worker produces tens and hundreds of times more products. An irresponsible or inebriated worker, on the other hand, who produces massive quantities of defective products, who cripples valuable machinery, who causes an industrial animal husbandry complex to be put out of commission, or who permits trains to collide, exceeds even scores and hundreds of times the damage caused by the Herostratuses of bygone days.

Technical inputs per worker will grow at an even faster rate in the future. After all, the party considers raising the effectiveness of the economy's development on the basis of the acceleration of scientific-technological progress, the technical retooling and reconstruction of production, and the intensive use of the existing production potential to be the principal task of the Twelfth Five-Year Plan. Thus, higher demands will be made not only on workers' skill levels, but also on such qualities as reliability, responsibility for the assigned task, the ability to make independent decisions, initiative, orderliness, decency, concurrence with the interests of the collective, and the readiness to perform their social duty.

Another reason for the heightened attention to the human factor in production is that human live labor in the last few years has become the weak link in the functioning of sophisticated technological systems. Man simply is not attaining the "pedestal" that scientific and technological progress ties to place him on. He neither can nor does he wish to satisfy the growing demands that are made upon him by production. There are many examples testifying to this, and the periodical press constantly cites new ones. For example, passenger and freight trains collided at the Barabinsk station [in Novosibirsk Region] in October

1984 because four skilled and experienced railroaders almost simultaneously violated eight different rules. Each violation seemed inconsequential by itself, but in their aggregate they were catastophic.[1] While this is not an everyday occurrence, there are combines in production that cannot harvest grain; there is footwear that is sent to the retail store as discounted goods almost the instant it comes off the production line. One recalls the many years of struggle waged by a departmental design office against a promising innovation that was born beyond its walls and that threatened to destroy its monopoly. . . . It seems that a person who for some reason gets out from under society's control and who is left on his own is still far from able to rise to the demands that are made upon him by today's productive forces. This lends special timeliness to the principle embedded in the party program that we must raise the social prestige of conscientious, high-quality labor and professional skill and that we must inculcate in every person a feeling of personal responsibility to society for the results of his labor.

The need for this is indeed enormous. But what should be done now, at a time when the education of the more perfect person is still not bearing the proper fruit?

One means of resolving this problem is the all-around strengthening of discipline—labor, technological, plan, and financial discipline—which presupposes the considerably more rigorous accounting and monitoring of all types of economic activity. But scientific-technological progress, by increasing the scale of utilized machinery, spatially separates people and individualizes work stations. The modern tractor driver in fact cultivates a vast field all by himself. A weaver or spinner tends dozens of looms, and it is impossible for an outsider to monitor the quality of their work. What is more, there is increasing division and specialization of labor, and the people who perform the most important jobs are the best, if not the only, specialists in their fields. Who is competent to monitor their work? Another question of no little importance is the subordination of quality control inspectors and the question of whether they have interests in common with the people whose work they inspect. People belonging to the same collective established personal contacts that compromise the objectivity of their monitoring of one another. In order to avoid a conspiracy between inspectors and the people whose work they inspect, "second—order inspectors" must be installed above them. This ultimately leads to an unwieldy, ineffective bureaucratic structure and, moreover, the number of "chiefs" per "indian" increases severalfold. Thus, the important consideration un-

der modern conditions is not so much externally monitoring the observance of the "letter of the instructions," even though this is still
essential, as the conscientious self-monitoring of skilled workers who
consider themselves professionals and who consider shoddy work inadmissible. Such a formulation of the questions returns us to the problem
of a person's social qualities.

The country's rapid social and economic development in the postwar
period produced substantial change in these qualities. With the systematic rise in the level of compulsory education, each new generation has
and continues to embark on its working career with a higher basic
educational level than its predecessor. The cultural level of the population is now appreciably higher. The development of the mass media,
especially television, newspapers, and magazines, has greatly broadened the population's outlook and made it better informed on events at
home and abroad. The system of people's value orientations has become more complex, and personality types have become more diverse.
The structure of needs and interests is now more highly individualized,
the legal and personal self-awareness of the working people has developed, their skill level has risen, and their labor and intellectual potential has increased.

The social qualities of the majority of the masses participating in the
economy would clearly seem to have grown. After all, better educated,
more cultured, and more highly skilled workers should obviously be
more aware and responsible, should have a deeper understanding of the
essence of social interests, and should strive to observe them. But life
does not run in a straight line, and the actual effect of people's social
development is more complex. Of course, most working people are
becoming increasingly aware and hence more attuned to social interests. But this is, first, not a unidirectional, but quite a contradictory,
process. Second—and this is to us the most important consideration—a
highly skilled, socially developed person is less amenable to administrative (and all the more so, bureaucratic) management. This is one of
the reasons why the methods of bureaucratic-directive management of
the economy and other spheres of life are becoming less effective.

The relaxation of the economic and legal "levers" that used to
compel people to conform regardless of their personal aspirations and
interests also operates in this direction. Let us recall the early postwar
years. The average level of the population's personal income was only
slightly higher than the subsistence level at that time. The principle
"who does not work, neither shall he eat" was followed almost literal-

ly, and the work of every mature person was in full measure the condition to the normal existence of the family. It was much more difficult to change jobs than it is today. Young people on collective farms, for example, had to have the permission of a general meeting of farm members before they could enroll in a technicum or institution of higher education.

The situation has dramatically changed since then. The average level of the population's income substantially exceeds the costs of the physiologically necessary means of subsistence. State benefits were introduced for the aged, the temporarily disabled, and invalids. The existence of job vacancies in most branches, regions, and cities facilitates job changes, enables people to take a closer look at various types of jobs, to try out various occupations, and to redistribute their labor effects between social production, personal household plots, and home life.

As a result, a considerable number of people have the opportunity to choose between two work behavior strategies. The first is expressed by the formula "maximum income for maximum labor" and is characteristic of family contract laborers in agriculture, seasonal construction crews, owners of large personal household plots producing for market, artels of prospectors in the gold mining industry, etc. The other strategy is characterized by the formula "guaranteed income for minimum labor" and is characteristic of persons in poor health, working pensioners, mothers, young people living with their parents, etc. The majority of the population combines the two strategies depending on their personal preferences and circumstances.

The opportunity for people to vary the degree of their labor participation in production depending on external circumstances and personal orientations accords them more freedom, makes their lives easier, and therefore should be regarded as a social attainment of society. However, it reduces still more the effectiveness of the administrative management of labor. Under modern conditions, the organization of more and more specialized departments, the increasing complexity of their structure and expansion of their apparatus, and the avalanche-like increase in the number of orders and instructions not only do not actually make social development more systematic, but on the contrary make it less systematic. The reason for this is that in the labyrinth of numerous contradictory instructions, it is even easier for an intelligent person to find the mode of behavior that corresponds to his own interests.

It should also be noted that the orders and instructions characteristic of administrative forms of management usually regulate the activity of special organizations and official and occupational groups. The growth of the socialization of production, however, leads to the intensive development of inter-occupational and interorganization ties, the realization of which is assigned to certain categories of personnel. In their continuous interaction with one another they enter into both business and personal relationships. The result is the formation of groups of people working in different organizations and departments that are formally independent of one another but that are in fact connected by constant, very serious relationships. While these groups are informal, their structure and behavior are essentially not monitorable, and their influence on the development of the social economy is very great. Thus, materials in the press show that the great majority of the major violations of legality and social morality are committed specifically by such informal groups that unite workers belonging to various organizations and various levels of the hierarchy of management. Administrative methods of management are completely powerless in the face of such groups.

The task of making the transition to economic methods of management was advanced back in the mid-1960s, but has been addressed slowly and inconsistently. As a result, adverse trends and difficulties arose in the nation's development in the 1970s and early 1980s.

One such trend has been the decline of the general systematic character and manageability of social development, which has been manifested in the relaxation of plan discipline; difficulties in material-technical supply; the development of economic "shadow" relations; the expansion of certain sources of unearned income; increasing unevenness in the demographic development of the nation's regions and republics; the increasing incidence of alcoholism and drunkenness; the weakening of family ties, etc. The task of overcoming the lag of production relations behind the development of the productive forces, which was discussed at the most recent plenums of the CPSU Central Committee, has marked the effort of society to master these processes and to make them amenable to systematic management.

The increase in the share of passive workers (who base their behavior in social production on the principle "it's no concern of mine" and "I don't need more than the rest"), the spread of the "instrumental" attitude toward labor primarily as a means of obtaining the vital necessities, and the reorientation of the interests of some workers from the social to the personal and family sphere, from the creative to the consumer sphere, should be classified among the adverse trends in evidence during this period.

The key to overcoming these trends, to accelerating social and economic development, lies in man's creative activity as the agent of economic, political, social, and cultural activity. The awakening of the social energy of the masses and their transformation into the real masters of the entire social economy, into the principal force in the management of society, presupposes certain changes in social thinking. "The party's entire experience indicates that it is not enough to change the economy, management, and education. It is also necessary to change the way people think, to instill in them the desire and ability to think and work in the new way."[2] It seems to us that changing the idea that took root in the preceding period regarding man's role in the development of the economy should be an important part of the required restructuring of our thinking.

Labor resources or the human factor?

Recent party documents, including the new CPSU Program, continually emphasize the impossibility of attaining the goals outlined by the party without the intensification of the human factor. However, in the social consciousness there is still a strong stereotype that developed several decades ago and that reflects the previous level of our society's development. This stereotype typically views people primarily as conditions to the functioning and development of production. This view of the place of man in the economy is adequately expressed by the concept "labor resources." It should be noted that this concept has played a large, positive role in economic science and practice. For a number of decades, it was effectively used to study the formation, distribution, redistribution, and utilization of society's labor power and to develop and improve the methods used to control these processes. And this concept can still be used successfully today to resolve many problems associated with the national economy's labor supply. However, it becomes clearly insufficient for the general understanding of the place of people in production under modern conditions.

Indeed, the view of people as labor resources means equating them with such material and physical factors of production as machinery, raw materials, energy, etc. Under this approach, people are viewed not as conscious agents of labor and economic activity, but as objects of management. After all, resources are by their very nature passive: they do not set their own goals; they do not have personal needs and interests; they do not show initiative; and they do not engage in purposeful behavior. On the contrary, they are "formed," "distributed," and "used" by someone else on the basis of interests that are external to their own.

The approach to man as a specific production resource reflects a certain level of development of social consciousness that is based on the corresponding level of development of society proper. A characteristic feature of this approach is the idea that the basic goal of society is to increase the economic and production potential (the construction of communism's material-technological base) and that normal living and working conditions for people are the means of attaining this goal.

Hence the relatively narrow understanding of social tasks primarily as securing the normal conditions of reproduction of labor resources and satisfaction of the population's consumer needs by improving wages in social production, by organizing the supply of consumer goods, by building well-appointed housing and preschool institutions, and by developing the sociocultural infrastructure. The importance of these tasks is indisputable. Their realization is a most necessary condition to the heightened creative activity of the masses. But the realization of these tasks is not sufficient to awaken the social energy that is required for the actual acceleration of the nation' development. Indeed, one cannot fail to see that their content is not specific to socialism. Many far-sighted capitalist countries today show extraordinary "concern" for working and living conditions, for the health and well-being of their work force simply because it is good business to do so.

Socialist society can and should set itself fundamentally new, more complex and promising goals which no one has ever reached before. But before these goals can be formulated, it is first of all necessary to adopt a broader and more sophisticated view of the place of man in socialist production. According to this view, people are the active agents of social activity, the creators of material and physical conditions of their own life, and the driving force in the development of production relations. They consciously set goals that correspond to their value orientations and consciously choose the means of attaining them. In their activity, they take into account behavioral norms and rules, the extent of their rights and obligations, and their own personal and collective interests. While submitting for the most part to the dominance of the state and the organizations representing it, they continue to engage in their own activity, which exerts no little pressure on the country's social and economic development.

The labor resources concept is not sufficient to express such a view of the role of man. After all, people are not "formed," they are born and reared, they receive training, they upgrade their skills, they marry, and they bear children. They are not "distributed" between jobs, but rather, consciously choose their occupation, place of residence and work, and migrate from one branch and enterprise to another. Finally, they are not "utilized," but consciously work in the social and personal sectors of production with one or another degree of motivation and effectiveness and realize their occupational and intellectual potential to a greater or lesser degree.

The CPSU Program's use of the "human factor," a concept that is new to our science and practice, expressed the modern understanding of man's place in the economy.

Encyclopedic dictionaries define "factor" as a cause or driving force. Consequently, the "human factor" focuses attention on man's active, driving role in the economy, which corresponds most to the present level of development. On the one hand, the concept of the human factor in production is an enormous step forward compared with the labor resources concept. On the other hand, it reflects the limitations of our society's level of development, the fact that the improvement of man himself has not yet become society's principal task, the fact that man is regarded, if not as a resource, then as a factor in certain external processes.

Just what is the human factor in production, in the economy, in society? In our opinion, it is an aggregate, complexly structured actor in social life. In other words, it is a system of interacting classes, strata, and groups with different status whose activity and interaction promotes the progressive development of society.

From the standpoint of our approach, social development can no longer be regarded as a means of attaining economic objectives. On the contrary, the accelerated growth of the productive forces here is a condition to the attainment of a qualitatively new level of development of social relations, and consequently, of man himself.

Change in the traditional view of the correlation between economic and social goals of development also entails a shift in emphasis in problems of social policy. While the old view primarily emphasized people's need for the vital necessities, the new, broader approach places the main focus on the need for developmental creative activity, accurate social and political information, political and economic democracy, social respect, interesting contacts, and intensive intellectual life. The task of creating social conditions that fully reveal man's abilities and develop his creative activity as an actor in social life is internally inherent in, and exclusively characteristic of, socialism. Therefore, the relative significance of these tasks of social policy will grow as our society matures.

Both groups of tasks are well balanced in the new party program, which sets the goal of making substantial progress in attaining the "*total* well-being and free *all-around* development of *all* members of society" (Lenin). The first part of this goal is developing into a whole system of tasks associated with raising the real incomes of all strata and groups of the population, with the greater satisfaction of demand for diverse, high-quality goods, with the creation of a modern, highly developed service sphere, with the future development of housing construction, with the further development of housing construction, with the improvement of health care for the Soviet people, etc. The second part of the goal is concretized in a system of tasks that is associated with the development of the creative energy and initiative of the masses, the development of the people's socialist self-government, with the strengthening of the spirit of collectivism and comradely mutual aid, the development of genuinely socialist morality, and the multifaceted development of the individual. The solution of the first, more urgent, but at the same time simpler group of problems is regarded as a means, a path, and a prerequisite to the solution of the second, more complex and longer-term group of problems.

The task of the social activiation of the individual is important in all stages of socialism. However, it is especially important today because it is the key to the intensification of production. After all, the intensive development of the economy means nothing more nor less than producing more and better products with the same or lesser expenditure of resources. Neither nature nor technology can themselves be the source of this type of development. Only the human factor, in other words, people who have completely mobilized their creative energy, initiative, will, and self-discipline, can become its source. Increasing the activity of people employed in production and unleashing their energy—this is what is meant by the conversion of the economy to the intensive path of development.

But how can "labor resources" be transformed into an active, driving force in economic development? The improvement of social relationships is the principal avenue in this direction. After all, according to Karl Marx, the human individual is the "imprint" of all the social relationships in which he is involved. If the practical experience of a certain segment of people convinces its representatives that initiative is more frequently punished than rewarded, and that obedient, not creative, workers fare better, one can hardly expect active workers to predominate. If most working people do not in fact have disposal over the means of production and do not bear economic responsibility for the results of their work, they will hardly be inclined to display a proprietary attitude toward socialist property. In order that a person would develop the feeling of a proprietor, he must be made not only a formal co-proprietor of all public property, but must also be a real, albeit only partial, proprietor of the small sector in which he works: he must be given a certain freedom to choose the methods of meeting targets and improving technology; he must at the same time be given responsibility for and interest in the final results of his labor. It is not by chance that collective contractual relations based on these principles present a generally promising result.

CPSU documents clearly point out the directions in restructuring economic management that have the aim of improving the organization of production and increasing the activism and initiative of the working people. Their general content boils down to the gradual replacement of administrative methods of management by the economic regulation of economic activity through the system of plan norms based on the material responsibility and interest of work collectives. The consistent implementation of the indicated measures will mean the actual recognition of socialist work collectives as relatively independent actors in labor and economic activity.

It is very important to restructure social consciousness in order to promote the understanding that the acceleration of society's social and economic development is only possible by "winning" man over as an actor, by understanding his own goals, motivations, and interests. Marx noted that an idea invariably discredits itself the instant it becomes separate from interest. Therefore, people's behavior can be effectively regulated only when we have a good understanding of their needs and interests.

Unfortunately, our science has not as yet studied the category of interests sufficiently in either a theoretical or practical sense. What is more, the development of applied research on a complex, many-sided, and contradictory system of social and economic interests is to a certain degree hindered by simplistic theoretical ideas inherited from the recent past. Thus, in scientific, and especially propagandistic, literature there are still more frequent references to the community of interests of all classes, strata, and groups in Soviet society than to their contradictoriness and complexity. More frequently people write about the need to subordinate personal interests to social interests than the experience of integrating these interests and of using personal and collective interests to attain social goals. Applied sociological research on the interests of various social, territorial, departmental, and occupational groups is as yet too isolated to permit us to draw general conclusions.

Under these conditions, organizations frequently have to make managerial decisions in the face of insufficient information on the interests of probable behavior of groups affected by these decisions. As a result, people's reactions to managerial measures prove to be different than expected. The raising of the regional wage coefficient in the northern regions of Siberia in the late 1960s can be cited as an example of this situation. The assumption was that higher personnel turnover—highly detrimental to production—was due to the insufficiently high level of earnings and that raising the wage coefficient would stabilize the work force. However, following the wage increase, personnel turnover not only did not diminish but actually increased. The reason was that a large number of workers who went north with the aim of saving up to buy a house, a car, etc., were, under the new conditions, able to achieve this aim in an appreciably shorter time.

The attempt to move inhabitants of small rural settlements to collective and state farm centers was another example of a mistaken action that resulted from ignorance of the population's interests and needs. Planners believed that this measure would curb the population's migration from town to city; in reality, however, it increased such migration dramatically. The miscalculation was that the inhabitants of small villages, upon being uprooted from their homes, moved directly to the city rather than to the centers of their farms as the administrative organizations had assumed. These examples graphically show that the effective management of economic and social development requires reliable knowledge of the behavioral patterns (motivations, interests, conditions) of the managed groups.

Mass activity and social justice

The new CPSU Program identifies as one of the tasks of social policy the more complete implementation of the principle of social justice in all basic spheres of social relations. The choice of this goal would seem to be extremely timely, since its realization would have the strongest impact on the development of the working people's initiative. But what is social justice? What does this concept mean under modern conditions? Can the level of social justice in society be measured? And what are the specific tasks in this area?

It should be noted first of all that the concept of social justice is of a historically concrete nature. Under socialism, this means above all the consistent and invariable observance of the principle: "From each according to his abilities, to each according to his labor." It seems to us that the social content of this formula is frequently diminished by the emphasis that is placed on its second part while the first remains in the shadows. What is more, this second part of the formula is understood simplistically, as merely an indication of the mode of income distribution. At the same time, with a sufficiently broad interpretation, the laconic formula of socialist relations acquire a very rich, multifaceted and a contemporary content that is closely associated with the question of social justice. Let us see what it consists of.

At least three conditions must be met so that every member of society would work according to his abilities. First, children that are born to families of different social standing must have, if not equal, then sufficiently similar "starting conditions" for the development of their abilities. This presupposes that republics, regions, cities, and villages have approximately the same kindergarten and day-care nursery accommodations, that the quality of preschool and other preparation of children for school is similar, that the quality of instruction in urban and rural, in capital and provincial schools, is similar, and consequently, that the graduates of all types of schools have the opportunity to continue their studies in technicums and higher education institutions in any, including the most prestigious, specialty. Also included here should be the equal opportunity of all young people having the appropriate abilities to receive an education in sports, art, and music. The aggregate of these conditions means that all representatives of every generation are guaranteed the opportunity to develop their abilities and talents and to form their labor potential by the time they embark on their labor activity.

Much has been done to create these conditions during the years of Soviet power. It is sufficient to recall the introduction of compulsory and complete secondary education, the creation of a broad network of higher education institutions, technicums, and vocational-technical training schools, and the development of many millions of children of peasants and workers into members of the national intelligentsia. But the existing level of society's development is not sufficient for the full realization of the principle "From each according to his abilities." The possibility of identifying and developing the abilities of children and adolescents in good time depends substantially on where they live (city or village, center or province) and on the socioeconomic status of their parents (income level, place in the structure of management, social connections). What is more, the higher the level of education (kindergarten, school, technicum, higher education institution), the greater are the differences between social groups in the share of those involved. Thus, in the past, the majority of students in the most prestigious institutions of higher education were graduates of a limited number of the best schools in the capital.

The second condition to working according to one's abilities is the dependence of the chance of getting blue-collar and official jobs in various spheres of the economy, in branches, at enterprises, etc., primarily on the personal labor potential of workers. We understand personal labor potential to mean the entire aggregate of qualities that make a person able to perform a specific type of work: state of health, physical strength, education, skill level, level of mental development, time on the job in a certain occupation, and, last but not least, the talent for a specific type of work. The demand to distribute jobs with due regard to the personal work potential of the workers must be realized not only with regard to young specialists but also in the workers' movement through various levels of their careers.

In general features, our social practice is organized in accordance with this condition, but it is still too early to speak of its consistent observance. It would be sufficient to point out the fact that the qualitative structure of jobs in economic zones, cities, and villages differs substantially. For example, a large number of the female graduates of rural schools who desire to remain in the countryside are compelled to become milkmaids because there are no other jobs for them. Their urban peers, on the other hand, have a broad choice of occupations. The great majority of the men living in mining industry settlements work in mines and quarries. It is extremely difficult for women to find work there. The need to overcome social and territorial differences, which lately have intensified, has been repeatedly emphasized in party and government documents. But this will unquestionably take considerable time. It will be still more difficult to overcome the influence of other factors hindering the consistent distribution of jobs depending on the workers' labor potential.

The third condition to the implementation of the principle "From each according to his abilities" is to give all workers the real possibility of working with maximum effect to the full extent of their powers. This means organizing the work in such a way that the end results of the work would depend primarily on the workers themselves, their knowledge, their abilities, their volitional qualities, etc. Workers who systematically stand idle due to the lack of raw materials, power, and spare parts; teachers who are unable to teach the way they consider necessary and correct; scientists whose research projects are shut down on the eve of their completion; actors who for years do not receive roles appropriate to their talents; enterprising managers who are bound hand and foot by instructions that prevent businesslike activity—all work below their ability. Their labor and creative activity is underutilized by society and they derive no satisfaction from their work.

The creation of material, economic, and social conditions for the more complete self-realization of society's members in labor activity is a task of both exceptional importance and extraordinary complexity. It can be resolved only gradually in the general process of socialist development. For quite a long time, the real possibilities of creative labor, for economic initiative, and for the active search for new technological, organizational, and socioeconomic decisions will in one way or another be "distributed" between groups of workers. And in order to be more just, this "distribution" must be based on objective criteria, must be carried out publicly, and must be the subject of broad, open discussion.

Such is the specific social content of the principle "From each according to his abilities." The consistent implementation of the principle "To each according to his labor" also requires a number of conditions. The first and most obvious condition is that the distribution of income (primarily wages) must correspond as closely as possible to the quantity and quality of the workers' labor. By establishing a normative level of pay for various types of labor, the state (in the person of its agencies) takes into account its strenuousness, the physical and nervous stress it entails, its complexity, its responsibility, danger, and the hazard it presents to health. Added to these qualities are the national economic significance of the branch (in practice—the "weight" and influence of a department), the degree of development and remoteness of an area, the acuteness of the personnel shortage, and certain other factors. Of course, it is difficult to measure all these qualities of labor precisely. It is still more difficult to compare them correctly with one another and to adduce the general correlation of remuneration of types of labor that differ on the basis of many criteria. This is one of the reasons for the frequent disparity between pay and the quantity and quality of labor expended by individual categories of workers.

Of course, the principle ''To each according to his labor'' refers not only to wages and not even only to monetary income, but to the aggregate of all material and social goods distributed in society. First of all, the principle of correspondence of income to labor inputs should be observed not only in the social, but also the personal sector of production, i.e., it should extend to individual labor activity (working personal household plots, rendering personal services to the population, individual construction of housing and farm buildings, handicrafts, etc.). At the same time, the actual profitability of these activities is determined not by wage policy but by the state of the consumer market, by the ratio of supply and demand for various goods and services. As a result, unearned income accumulates among certain groups of the population. For example, the owners of private plots in southern regions with unique climatic conditions appropriate the bulk of the differential rent in addition to their earned income.

Certain groups of workers use their official right to dispose of public property as a source of unearned income for selfish purposes. We refer to shady commercial transactions, to speculation in scarce goods, to rendering official ''services'' to subordinate and allied organizations for the corresponding remuneration, etc. Such phenomena are fundamentally inimical not only to the idea of social justice but also to the idea of socialism in general, and therefore deserve to be combated mercilessly by all the people. The CPSU Program states that the party will take all necessary measures to protect socialist property, to halt all attempts to use it for selfish ends, and to eradicate forms of appropriation that are alien to socialism. But to date it must be admitted that the principle ''To each according to his labor'' has been carried out incompletely and inconsistently.

Adequate social security for the non-able-bodied population from social consumption funds is the second condition to the realization of this principle. After all, society is interested in maintaining a population of normal size and age structure and in securing the requisite birth rate. And if this is the case, the economic costs of raising children must to a certain degree be distributed between the parents and the state. Nor do pensions for persons beyond working age contradict the principle of distribution according to one's labor. First, these people have expended their labor potential in the nation's social production, have promoted the development of its economy, and are now entitled to receive an income for their previous labor services. Second, justified old age pensions place young families that have and do not have elderly relatives in more equitable conditions. It is not by chance that the Twelfth Five-Year Plan earmarks higher payments to pensioners in the lowest payment groups.

The third condition to distribution according to one's labor understood in the broad sense of the term involves the transformation of the population's money incomes into tangible material and social assets, i.e., the supply of goods and services. In socialist society, where most of the population's income is earned, the possibility of converting money into material and social assets must in principle be the same for all. This applies not only to trade in foodstuffs, fashionable clothing, and durable goods, but also to the purchase of cooperative housing, to the construction of personal garages, and to the distribution of tourism and sanatorium vouchers. The realization of this condition presupposes both a similar level of supply of goods to all settlements and the open nature of trade in all types of consumer goods.

At the present time, two principal circumstances hinder the realization of these conditions. The first is the imbalance between the supply of consumer goods and the population's effective demand and the scarcity of many goods. The free, uncontrolled sale of goods that are in higher demand would place trade personnel and the least employed segment of the population that can shop frequently in a favored position. The controlled distribution of such goods is organized in such a way as to favor those who work intensively.

The second circumstance, hindering free trade in all types of consumer goods, including housing, travel accommodations, etc., is the continued existence of groups living on unearned income in our society. The CPSU poses the task of consistently striving to see to it that the distribution mechanism would be a reliable obstacle to unearned income, to wage leveling, to everything that contradicts the norms and principles of socialist society. As long as these phenomena exist, however, the controlled distribution of scarce goods will be one way of attenuating them. However, this, in turn, generates a certain measure of injustice and, hence, should be viewed only as a temporary measure.

In describing the specific content of the main principle of socialism, we have at the same time also tried to describe the basic direction of increasing the justice of social relations. When we examine these directions, we must remember that the concept of social justice has its "objective" and "subjective" aspects. The first reflects the degree to which the system of social relations in a specific stage of development corresponds to the theoretical model of socialism, while the second is the subjective evaluations of the justice of social relations by various groups and strata. While coinciding in the main, these evaluations may be substantially at variance with one another in individual instances.

One reason for this is that the content of the principle "From each according to his ability, to each according to his labor," even in the broadest interpretation, does not encompass the entire sphere of social relations. People who are involved in the entire system of social relations may also encounter injustice in such areas that are not directly embraced by the socialist formula. They include, for example, such phenomena as the bureaucratic examination of the working people's declarations and petitions; the routing of complaints to be examined by the person against whom they are lodged; incorrect, prejudiced judicial proceedings; the unjustified inclusion of high-ranking authorities in creative collectives entitled to state bonuses, etc. People who encounter such phenomena take them as a serious social injustice, which has a direct impact on their behavior.

The status and interests of the corresponding social groups are the second source of discrepancy between "objective" and subjective evaluations of social justice. Since people's thinking is determined by their experience, various groups' views of justice are not impartial: as a rule, they are "colored" by certain interests. Therefore, one and the same phenomenon (the relative pay of various categories of personnel, the way in which scarce goods are distributed, one or another management decision) is frequently perceived by one group as correct and by another as unjust. Assessments of social justice are also affected by differences in the personal views, upbringing, practical experience, and value orientations of people.

Group behavior is directly regulated not by the objective level of social justice but by the subjective reflection of this level in mass consciousness. The masses' confidence in the progressive character and justice of their social system is a key source of their creative energy, labor enthusiasm, and economic initiative. On the other hand, frequent encounters with injustice, with discrepancies between actions and words, with the defenselessness of good and impunity of evil generate disappointment with social values, indifference, and people's retreat into their personal interests. At best, this results in social passivity; at worst, in depravity and antisocial behavior.

The foregoing attests to the importance of applied sociological research on people's views of social justice. Such research will make it possible to elicit the "sore points" of various groups and strata in this area, to elaborate effective measures of improving social relations.

We note in conclusion that the incomplete justice of relations in our society is due to both economic and social factors. The former reflect the deficient level of development of the productive forces, which restricts the potential for the more uniform distribution of many goods; the latter—the reluctance of social groups that for certain reasons enjoy inordinate privileges to give them up willingly.

The strengthening of social justice is a complex social process that takes place through the struggle of interests of different social groups and strata. Under these conditions, it is especially important to expand the possibility of work collectives and occupational and territorial groups to openly express, discuss, and defend their interests at various levels of management and to receive clear answers to their demands. The expansion of such opportunities is directly tied in with the strengthening of socialist democracy, with the expanded participation of the working people in management. In combination with the more consistent implementations of the principle of social justice, this is the most reliable means of accelerating social and economic progress.

Notes

1. *Literaturnaia gazeta*, October 31, 1985.
2. M. S. Gorbachev, *Korennoi vopros ekonomicheskoi politiki partii*, Moscow, Politizdat, 1985, p. 29.

6 Social Justice and the Human Factor in Economic Development

The party links the acceleration of the country's socioeconomic development first and foremost with raising the creative activity of the masses. The successful implementation of this policy presupposes a clear understanding of the processes that have generated substantially greater attention to the human factor and to social questions. What is the content of these processes?

Scientific-technological progress, particularly such of its manifestations as the increase in machines per worker, the increased specialization of labor, and the actual growth of the socialization of production, is the principal cause of the objective increase in the role of the human factor in production. All these processes—each through its own mechanism—operate in the same direction.

With the growth of machinery use, every worker brings into play an ever greater mass of means of production, the value of which is transferred to the product. As a result, living labor is in a sense multiplied by a continuously growing coefficient that reflects the value of the technical means used. In certain kinds of highly mechanized production, the cost of the machinery is several times higher than the lifetime earnings of a worker in this production. Under these conditions, there are qualitative changes in the criteria society uses to evaluate labor: while the effectiveness of labor was previously measured primarily in

"Chelovecheskii faktor razvitiia ekonomiki i sotsial'naia spravedlivost'," *Kommunist*, 1986, no. 13, pp. 61–73. Russian text © 1986 by "Pravda" Publishers, the publishing house of the Central Committee of the CPSU. *Kommunist* is the theoretical and political journal of the Central Committee of the CPSU. Translation © 1987 by M. E. Sharpe, Inc. Translated by arrangement with VAAP, the USSR Copyright Agency. Translated by Arlo Schultz.

the value of its output, no less important today are the integrity and effective use of means of production and the economical expenditure of power, raw materials, and supplies. The high level of capital per worker makes workers' lack of skills, thoughtlessness, and irresponsibility tens and hundreds of times costlier. It is sufficient to recall that the direct damage from the accident at the Chernobyl Atomic Power Plant, which was due to human error, is estimated at almost two billion rubles, and loss of human life and health cannot be assessed in economic terms. This tragic event is just the most obvious evidence of the significance of the human factor—in both a positive and, unfortunately, negative sense as well—under the conditions of the scientific-technological revolution.

The growing specialization of social labor has a considerable impact on the phenomenon under review. One of its most important consequences is the emergence and gradual intensification of "monopolistic effects" in production and in research and development. Industrial giants that have no competitors dictate their own delivery terms to their customers and even go as far as foisting on them products that are easier to produce. Departmental institutes keep valuable inventions by "outside" scientists out of "their" branch for years and decades. As a result, society is increasingly dependent on the personal qualities—honesty, decency, dedication to society's interests—of economic managers and engineering-technical personnel. A similar situation is developing in the workplace. With the increasing complexity of the content of labor, it has become more and more difficult to monitor its quality—after all, the person doing the monitoring must understand the job at least as well as the person performing it. But it is unprofitable and extremely ineffective to divert a large number of skilled workers to monitoring the activity of others. There is but one truly promising solution: the inculcation of all categories of workers with the capacity for self-monitoring based on a high degree of professionalism, personal dignity, pride in the excellent quality of job performance, and an aversion to careless work.

Finally, the role of the human factor is also rising in connection with the increase in the actual socialization of production, in particular, with the accelerating increase in the number of economic relationships (at the present time, there are more than five hundred billion economic transactions in the nation every year). The role of automatic regulators of these relationships in a socialist economy is limited, their formation is of a planned nature, and the personnel of planning, financial, and other management organs are responsible for them. Quality, responsibility, the initiative-oriented character of their activity, and the understanding of social interests or, conversely, indifference to them, exert an ever increasing influence on the effectiveness of a socialist economy. Hence, here too, the question is primarily one of man and his social qualities, without the improvement of which acceleration can hardly be attained.

All the described processes are objective and in the future will only intensify, which makes the effective management of the human factor in production especially important. At the same time, the social conditions of this management are also undergoing appreciable change.

First of all, there has been a change in the object of management *per se*: the level of education, culture, knowledgeability, and legal and personal awareness of the working people is rising with every five-year plan. Their interests and needs are becoming more and more complex, and their personality types are becoming increasingly diverse. As people's educational level rises and their general outlook broadens, they strive for a greater degree of independence in their work, for an active part in the decision-making process, and for the unleashing of their own creative potential. If this striving is not realized, people frequently become alienated from work and turn their interests to other spheres. Thus, while a socially developed person unquestionably possesses greater labor potential, he is at the same time unquestionably more difficult to control.

As regards change in the social conditions of controlling the economic behavior of people, the most important consideration here is probably the relaxation of administrative and economic pressure to perform intensive labor in social production. The rise of the general standard of living and the development of social guarantees in the spheres of education, medicine, and housing have reduced the economic necessity for such labor and enable workers to try their hand at different occupations for quite a long time, to devote a considerable time to individual labor activity, to their household, etc. At the same time, the existence of job vacancies in most regions and cities makes it possible in principle for people to earn quite handsomely without overly exerting themselves. Characteristically, 27 percent of managers of industrial enterprises in the Altai consider the strained labor picture and the "competition" of enterprises for manpower to be the principal reason why the work force is not more active.[1]

The behavior of people in the formation and distribution of earned income today varies. Some social and occupational groups (seasonal brigades, gold prospecting artels, families working under collective contracts) strive primarily to maximize their earnings, for the sake of which they are ready to work without regard to time or even their health. On the other hand, others (the elderly, boys and girls still living at home) prefer low earnings and a limited work schedule. The relative value assigned to additional income or leisure time is the criterion of choice. To many, these values are comparable. Thus, according to one sociological study, workers who are members of progressive brigades listed cash bonuses as the most important incentive (all 100 percent of the respondents listed them in first place); the second most important incentive was additional leave time (83 percent).[2] The increasing value of leisure time is also attested to by the fact that the majority of those quitting their jobs are in no hurry to start their new job and usually use the interval to make repairs on their apartment, to perform household work, to visit relatives, and frequently to go on vacation.

Obviously, the only system that can be effective today is the one that is based on the precise knowledge and able use of the workers' interests. And since these interests are many-sided, depend on a multitude of factors, and change under the influence of circumstances, the management of the human factor must be distinguished by a diversity of methods, by flexibility, and by sensitivity to local conditions and dynamic changes. Methods approved once and for all time are [eventually] contraindicated—after all, flows of uncontrolled activity invariably blaze a trail between the boulders of obsolete instructions. The range of the arsenal of means used as incentives and "disincentives" is also of no little importance. If they are only reduced to the "ruble" and to administrative prohibitions on certain modes of behavior, the considerable and sometimes most important part of the interests of the work force will remain outside the sphere of administrative influence.

Shortcomings in the existing system of management of the human factor (about which much has been said in party documents of late) and its lack of correspondence to the new social situation have led to theinsufficiently effective use of society's social resources and labor potential. Sociological research on the industry and agriculture of various regions of the country shows that scarcely one-third of the nation's labor force is working at full capacity. The rest of the labor force, by its own admission, is working below full capacity and could do more and better work if production was otherwise organized. This was the opinion expressed by 80 percent of agricultural specialists, 78 percent of middle management, as well as by state farm workers and collective farmers in rural areas of the Altai. The share of those working at full capacity on the economically strong farms is higher. The corresponding share on economically weak farms is lower. But the difference is by no means as great as might have been expected: 32 percent and 17 percent. It turns out that even on the best farms, two-thirds of the labor force are working at less than full capacity. The reasons they give are: poor organization of labor, weaknesses in the system of incentives, and the ineffectiveness of the administrative management of production. The following fact is also illustrative: middle managers on Altai collective and state farms were asked whether their subdivisions had sufficient manpower: 65 percent answered in the negative, 32 percent essentially answered in the affirmative, and 3 percent stated that they had a manpower surplus. Then the same managers were asked how the situation would change if they were given the right to regulate their own work force, the work load, and the pay of their personnel within the limits of the allocated fund. Forty-two percent replied that in such a case some of the work force (15–20 percent on the average) would become surplus.

This problem also has a qualitative aspect that is associated with the utilization of the professional knowledge, skills, and experience of people. It is paradoxical that in our reality, engineering-technical personnel perform the labor of skilled workers, and that managers do not try to climb the career ladder and broaden the scope of their activity, but on the contrary, try to make it narrower. As our research showed, only 9 percent of Siberian collective and state farm managers and 13 percent of middle-level managers would like to occupy a higher position in the future, while 30 percent and 72 percent, respectively, would prefer to work in lower positions. And this is not because the people do not like or cannot cope with their work, but is rather because society's evaluation of their work does not correspond to its actual level of difficulty. The transformation of qualified engineers into workers and economic managers into subordinates confirms the inability of the existing system of management to secure the effective functioning of society's social resources.

What does this lead to? One of the results observed in recent five-year plans has been the lowering of the planned character of social and economic development, of the degree of plan fulfillment, and of the attainment of goals. In the economic area, the slackening of the actual growth rates of production in various branches has as a rule brought about the lowering of plan indicators in the next five-year plan. Such was the case in agriculture, for example, where the planned gross output growth rate declined from 25 percent in the Eighth to 13 percent in the Eleventh Five-Year Plan. The actual production growth rates declined from 21 to 5.5 percent during that period. In sum, despite the systematic lowering of the branch's output growth plans, the degree of their fulfillment declined from 84 to 59 percent under the Eighth and Ninth to 56 and 46 percent under the Tenth and Eleventh five-year plans. Clearly, such dynamics could not be the result of conscious planning, and the plans only passively recorded the spontaneous development of adverse factors. The increasingly common practice of adjusting annual plans downward, the systematic nonfulfillment of five-year plans by a number of branches, the imbalance of production plans with respect to resources, the disharmony of material-technical supply, the development of economic "shadow" relations, etc., should be classified among the manifestations of spontaneity.

A similar trend has also been evident in the social development of society. For example, the unevenness in the social development of individual republics and regions, of large cities and small towns, of central and peripheral villages has not only not diminished but has even increased. So it is that the task that has been advanced in the course of several five-year plan periods—that of placing greater emphasis on the improvement of living conditions in newly developed regions in Siberia compared with already developed regions—has not been realized in practice. For example, in 1984 nine out of eleven regions and territories in Siberia were identified as regions of Russia with the worst housing conditions; in six of these regions, meat consumption was lower than the republic average. It is typical that in comparing housing conditions just with Novosibirsk (to say nothing of other Siberian cities), the population of European Russia, the Ukraine, Moldavia, the Baltic, and Belorussia enjoys 20–23 percent more living space per person, which can serve as an indicator of general regional differences in the quality of life. All these facts show that the organs of government in recent years have not by any means always been able to maintain a genuine planned socioeconomic development of society.

As noted in the documents of the [Twenty-seventh] Congress, in order to put a definite end to adverse trends in the development of the economy, to make the economy highly dynamic, and to open the door to truly revolutionary reforms in a short period of time, the party deems it essential to include the broad masses of working people in these processes and to arouse their social activism, energy, and initiative. This means above all the consistent, in-depth, all-around coordination of the personal interests of workers with collective interests, and collective interests with social interests.

As is known, the economic mechanism of the economy's management and the party's social policy serve this task in the socioeconomic sphere. The economic mechanism determines the forms of organization, planning, and stimulation of economic activity. It places every category of workers in certain organizational and economic conditions and thereby shapes its economic interests (for example, the collective forms of organization and stimulation of labor motivate people to obtain maximum output for minimum inputs). Social policy—well-thought out, tested, carefully balanced, and whole—is the most powerful means of generating not only the material but also nonmaterial and personal interest of the masses in attaining social goals, and is the main source of social and labor enthusiasm.

Social policy embraces the activity of the party and the state in the management of society's social structure, i.e., in the regulation of the status, relationships, and interaction of basic social groups. In this connection, it should be noted that the social group is a central sociological concept. It is generic to such concepts as class, social stratum, territorial community, occupational category, work collective, etc. (We recall Lenin's definition of classes as large groups of people that differ in their place in the historically concrete mode of production). As is known, the largest groups in society are classes, nations, and nationalities; the urban and rural population; and representatives of physical and mental labor. While coordinating the basic interests of these groups is a necessary condition to the normal development of society, this is by no means enough for the resolution of modern problems. The economic mechanism in combination with social policy is called upon to coordinate and properly direct the interests of groups representing different departments, branches of the national economy, types of enterprises, regions, and types of settlements (for example, old and new, large and small cities; urban, and rural-type settlements; large and small villages). Nor does this tell the entire story, since the broadly construed social structure of society includes groups of workers categorized by occupation, skill level, and position, population groups in various types of employment (workers in social production, students and pupils, housewives, pensioners, persons working in the home), social-demographic groups, etc. Substantive differences in certain aspects of the status of groups in society—character of labor, place in the management of the economy and society, level and structure of income, place of residence, affiliation with one or another nationality, etc.—are the general criterion on the basis of which groups are differentiated. After all, groups that have different statuses usually have different interests, the coordination of which with one another as well as with the interests of society is the goal of policy.

The CPSU program sets out four basic goals for the party's social policy: (1) the steady improvement of the Soviet people's living and working conditions; (2) the more complete realization of the principle of social justice in all spheres of social relations; (3) the reduction of distinctions between classes, social groups, and strata, and the elimination of essential distinctions between mental and physical labor and between town and country; and (4) the improvement of national relations and the strengthening of fraternal friendship between the country's nations and nationalities. These tasks are naturally interconnected, and moreover, some of them embody the final aims of the social development of society to a greater degree, while others embody the means of attaining these goals, which will have a very direct bearing on the intensification of the human factor.

The task of securing social justice in all spheres of social relations has evoked the active response of the people, because numerous elements of injustice accumulated in different spheres of our society's life in the course of several five-year plan periods preceding the Twenty-seventh CPSU Congress, and this circumstance was painfully perceived by the working people. Many facts of actual life in that period were at odds with socialist principles. Frequent clashes with various forms of social injustice and vain attempts at individual struggle against its manifestations became one of the principal causes of the working people's alienation from social goals and values. This is why the resolute struggle—in deeds, not words—against negative phenomena in this sphere, which can be overcome at the existing level of development of the productive forces, is the truest avenue to restoring the faith and the creative engagement of the masses today.

Wherein lies the content of the principle of social justice? Evidently, here it is also possible to speak of ends and means. In regard to the future development of socialist society, social justice is understood to mean the establishment of political, social, and economic equality of social groups, i.e., the realization of the social equality of their status, while a number of distinctions in its concrete manifestations continue. But as regards the present, we are speaking about *socialist* justice (it was not by chance that this term was used in the congress materials). The socioeconomic aspect of socialist justice, the basic content of which is the consistent implementation of the principle "from each according to his ability, to each according to his labor," is most important for the effective functioning of the human factor in production. Socialist justice consists, first, in the encouragement and all-around support of those groups that make the most important contribution to social development and that use all their energy and capacities to this end; and, second, in the social control and economic regulation of the status of groups that place their narrow professional, departmental, or local interests above social interests to the detriment of social development.

The bulk of the working people employed in social production are unquestionably the party's social base of support in the struggle for the restructuring of production relations and the acceleration of the country's development. Although workers, managers, and specialists have different statuses and have, in addition to the common features that unite them, a number of specific interests, they are all vitally interested in the acceleration of socioeconomic development, as this is a condition for the accelerated rise of the standard of living. Of course, workers in material production include active proponents of the new, people with initiative and enterprise, as well as those who are passive and conservative in their thinking. The former must be encouraged and supported in every way; they must have room for their creative aspirations. The advantages of the new relations must be proven to the latter; they must be imbued with their successive affirmation based on the practice of socialist justice relations.

In addition to those who completely link their well-being to social production, in our society, as already noted, there are people who are prepared to work very intensively, not under general conditions, but more for "number one"—under a family contract, on a personal household plot, in seasonal construction brigades, and in other types of piecework. The labor of these groups of the population is as a rule highly effective and moreover is often supplementary to their labor in social production. Therefore, society concludes a unique agreement with them under mutually advantageous conditions. Since labor in the individual sector of production does not require state capital investments, does not provide entitlement to social security from social funds, requires personal initiative, and entails economic risk, the average pay for this labor must obviously be significantly higher than wages in social production. However, an unduly high difference in income per unit of labor compared with social production can lead to the formation of a social stratum that has a disproportionately high share of society's wealth compared with the rest of the working people. Therefore, while favorable conditions are created for the effective economic activity of groups employed predominantly in the private sector of the economy, it is at the same time necessary to strictly take into account and monitor their incomes and to tax them progressively starting at a certain level.

Nor can we close our eyes to the fact that the actual status of certain categories of people makes their interests divergent from, and sometimes opposite to, society's interests. It is not by chance, for example, that there is such heated discussion today of bureaucrats who obviously do not desire to surrender their ''positions,'' who here and there impede and undermine progressive reforms, who stubbornly continue to place narrow departmental, local, and purely selfish interests above society's interests. Operators in the so-called shadow economy—large-scale and petty profiteers, secondhand dealers, brokers, etc.—are still numerous. Using the imperfections of the existing economic management mechanism, they extract their unearned and unlawful income from the ''pockets'' of both the population and the state. The periodical press cites numerous instances of ties between ''shady'' operators with corrupt state officials, and this is hardly by chance: the existence of such ties is the result of the prolonged, unhindered extraction of unlawful income.

Under these conditions, the state obviously cannot have as its goal the uniform enhancement of the degree of satisfaction of the needs of all elements of the social structure. The implementation of a strong social policy means the systematic differentiation of the growth of the well-being of population groups that differ substantially in their role in the socioeconomic development of society, that actively promote its acceleration, or conversely, that hinder it and make an uneven personal and collective contribution to the enhancement of the well-being of all society. It is precisely this differentiated approach that makes social policy *policy*.

Soviet society's attainments in the realization of social justice are obvious. They have been described in the scientific and political literature and conceptualized in the materials of the Congress. But the party orients us first and foremost toward the analysis of unresolved problems. Therefore, in my view it is important to determine the directions in the further strengthening and consolidation of socialist justice in the socioeconomic sphere. What are the conditions demanded for the consistent implementation of the principle "From each according to his abilities, to each according to his labor?"

It seems to us that three major conditions are required so that every adult member may work to the full measure of his abilities. First, the further equalization of the "starting" opportunities for the development of the abilities of people that belong to different social groups living in different regions of the country, in cities, in the countryside, etc. This requires the similar quality of preschool education of children in various types of institutions; the reduction of differences—based on the accelerated development of lagging links—in the level of knowledge conveyed by rural and urban, capital and provincial schools; and the equalization of the opportunity of various groups of youth to learn complex, interesting, and socially prestigious occupations. It is not so necessary to prove how difficult is this problem as it is to prove the necessity of solving it.

The second condition to labor based on one's abilities is the distribution of jobs in social production depending on the personal labor potential and business qualities of people. The difficulty is that over 30 percent of the work force in industry and 70 percent of the work force in agriculture is still performing simple manual labor, which does not correspond to the needs and abilities of a single social group. While the all-around reduction of semiskilled and heavy physical labor is an urgent task, it is being carried out slowly. No less important is the correct distribution of workers among existing places in social production, in particular, the movement of the most gifted workers with the corresponding professional qualities to places requiring complex and responsible labor. The present mechanism for placing and moving cadres in social production does not provide a sufficiently effective solution to this problem, and therefore it must be modernized and improved.

The third and final condition is the potential of all categories of personnel to work to the fullest of their ability in social production. This means that workers may work without forced idle time, without alternating periods of rush work and idleness; that economic managers can work without being hounded over petty details, with a sufficient degree of economic independence and responsibility. It means that specialists in the national economy have the right to creative search and to make independent decisions within the framework of their competence. It would seem that the interests of society and the individual coincide entirely on this question, but its practical resolution is difficult and requires considerable effort and time.

What has been said concerns the first part of the most important principle of socialism—labor according to one's ability (even though it does not exhaust the given problem). In my opinion, the realization of its second part—consistent distribution according to one's labor—presupposes five main conditions: (1) the approximate correspondence of the wage levels of various categories of workers to the quantity and quality of their labor, as well as to the relative cost of living in various regions of the nation; (2) the eradication of all unlawful income and a socially just level of income in the individual sector of production; (3) the unity of the country's consumer goods market, i.e., the equal availability of all types of commodities to all groups of working people, the equal purchasing power of the ruble no matter who earns it, and the approximate correspondence of prices on consumer goods to their social value (with the exception of the deliberate deviation of prices from value for the purpose of solving social problems); (4) the socially just distribution of the costs of caring for children, the aged, and invalids between the state and the population; and (5) the socially substantiated correlation between the distribution of consumer goods for money and free of charge.

The social program, which can be divided into minimum and maximum programs, is the concrete embodiment of the party's social policy applicable to a certain period of time. The goal of the minimum program, which is usually oriented toward the five-year period, is to satisfy the most important, urgent needs of the population and to correct the most obvious injustices in the distribution of material and social goods. The most important elements of such a program are reflected in the materials of the Twenty-seventh Congress and subsequent decrees on the plan for the economic and social development of the USSR in 1986–90. Much attention in the process was devoted to improving the conditions of education of the younger generation, to strengthening the material-technical base of school and vocational education, and to the improvement of the vocational guidance of school pupils. Serious reforms are planned in the conditions, character, and content of labor. The most obvious disproportions in the pay of various categories of workers are to be eliminated. Basic significance is attached to improving the circulation of consumer goods and services.

A system of measures for improving the status of nonworking groups of the population—pensioners, invalids, war and labor veterans, mothers—is scheduled for the Twelfth Five-Year Plan. Social consumption funds will grow at a slightly faster rate than the distribution fund based on labor; these funds will also finance the development of housing construction, public utilities and amenities, health care, the system of education, and socialist culture. On the whole, the social program of the Twelfth Five-Year Plan is quite intensive. At the same time, of course, it cannot solve the entire complex of problems relating to socialist justice.

In order to secure the more active participation of the masses in all spheres of social life, there must be more highly integrated, effective, and at the same time complex, measures requiring serious substantiation, which in their aggregate may comprise the content of a strategic social program aimed at attaining the fundamental goals of socialism, the full realization of socialist justice in all spheres of social life, and the creation of conditions for the social development of the representatives of all social groups. The basic directions and contours of this program are contained in the materials of the Twenty-seventh CPSU Congress, but their implementation requires the much more concrete critiquing of many questions on which [social] scientists are not as yet of one mind. The discussion of the corresponding problems in the press is thus all the more important.

In view of the limited framework of this article, I shall discuss only two problems of the long-range social program that strike me as particularly urgent and complex. The first of them is associated with the qualitative reform of the system of workplaces in social production and with the change in the conditions of employment.

The sharp acceleration of scientific-technological progress, which will inevitably entail serious reform of the system of workplaces in the national economy, is one of our society's pressing needs. Semiskilled manual labor already in the next few years will be more actively eliminated and replaced by skilled mechanized and automated labor. Such change in the structure of workplaces in some measure satisfies the working people's growing need for more challenging labor. But at the same time, millions of semiskilled workers will be released from the productive branches. Accordingly, we must even now (1) make reliable quantitative forecasts of the release of concrete categories of workers at the regional and branch level; and (2) search for the most economically and socially effective avenues of further utilization of these workers.

In the first stage, the task of finding jobs for released workers will be made easier by the low shift coefficient of equipment in most branches of industry and by the labor shortage in construction, agriculture, and branches of the nonproductive sphere: the number of job vacancies in the national economy is currently estimated in the hundreds of thousands and millions. But from a social standpoint, the redistribution of workers between branches and enterprises, between groups according to occupation and duties, and between regions and cities throughout the nation will entail considerable difficulty. The intensification of job change processes will obviously require an appreciable increase in the territorial and labor mobility of cadres and the psychological restructuring of groups of workers that have historically been highly stable. And since this takes time, there may possibly be an increase in branch and territorial disproportions between the demand for and supply of labor. The incomplete satisfaction of the manpower needs of some branches and regions will be combined with the difficulty of certain population groups in finding employment in others. In order to reduce these disproportions to a minimum, it is essential to identify and take into account categories of workers that are scheduled for release from production, to organize their retraining in new occupations, and to systematically redistribute them among new workplaces.

Workers who have the least value from the standpoint of work collectives, who are indifferent toward labor and product quality, and who take little part in public life, to say nothing about idlers, drunkards, rolling stones, etc., will unquestionably be the first to encounter the need to move to other branches of production that are faced with a manpower shortage, to move to other regions and cities. Such a situation will contribute to the growing social value of workplaces in social production, the strengthening of labor discipline, and the improvement of product quality. However, the possibility is not excluded that honest, conscientious, but undereducated people who are not ready for retraining (for example, people of pre-pension age and mothers of numerous children) may encounter difficulty finding jobs. They will have to receive both material and social aid, *inter alia*, through the development of types of work that can be done at home, part-time and flexible employment of housewives, the expansion of family and cooperative forms of labor activity, early retirement, etc. At the present time it is difficult to picture the entire complex of social problems associated with the acceleration of scientific-technological progress, to say nothing of suggesting measures for solving them. But it is important to investigate these problems.

The second group of long-term problems that I would like to address is associated with the need for comprehensive reform of the national economy's wage system, of retail prices on consumer goods and services, and mechanisms for the distribution of goods from social consumption funds. The urgency of such a reform is determined (1) by the substantial divergence between the labor and income of many categories of workers; (2) by the economically and socially unsubstantiated deviation of prices and rates on many consumer goods from their social value; and (3) by the lack of sufficiently clear and substantiated principles governing the division of paid and unpaid distribution of goods.

The current wage reform can only eliminate the most flagrant and obvious disproportions. The less significant discrepancies between labor and consumption, however, gradually accumulate and increasingly deform the wage system throughout the nation. Therefore, it presently needs not partial correction and improvement, but fundamental, basic restructuring. In order to implement such restructuring, it is necessary not only to make a true determination and to experimentally verify socially substantiated correlations in the remuneration of the most important types of labor, but also to accumulate financial reserves, thereby making it possible to raise the pay of workers belonging to certain categories without infringing the interests of others. This problem can be resolved more effectively and promptly in complex with the reform of retail prices and the terms under which services are offered.

But why must prices of consumer goods be reformed in general, particularly at the same time that wages are reformed? The point is that these levers for the distribution and redistribution of the population's personal incomes are closely connected, and the final proportions of consumption form under the joint influence of both of them. As is known, when distribution is based on labor, "each individual producer receives back from society as much as he gave it, minus all deductions" (Karl Marx and Friedrich Engels, *Works* [in Russian], vol. 19, p. 18). At the same time, wages are the monetary equivalent of labor, and the prices of goods received are the latter's monetary equivalent. The substantial deviation of retail prices from the social value of products under these conditions means the concealed redistribution of income according to criteria that lie not in the labor sphere but in the structure of personal consumption. The socialist state actively uses this mode of income redistribution for social goals. Thus, motor vehicles, luxury items, and wines and spirits are understandably sold for much more than their cost, while books, phonograph records, and children's toys are sold for less, thereby stimulating their consumption and making them more accessible to the population.

However, not all deviations of price from value can be considered socially justified. Let us take as an example meat and dairy products, the retail prices on which are maintained by the state at a level that is far below the enterprise cost of production. Meat combines and dairy plants purchase livestock and milk for prices that for the most part make their production profitable for collective and state farms. They sell the finished product to trade enterprises for much lower prices. The difference, which amounts to 40–50 billion rubles, is covered by the state budget. As a result, a very appreciable part of the population's general consumption fund is distributed not on the basis of labor or need, but as a subsidy to those groups of the population that purchase the indicated products in state stores. Nevertheless, there are still meat and dairy product shortages in many regions of the nation. Trade operations in rural areas and small towns are for the most part performed by consumer cooperative stores whose prices are higher. It would obviously be more correct to sell meat and milk on the basis of their social cost, thereby placing all social groups in an equal position from the standpoint of obtaining them.

In my view, the differentiation of prices on high- and low-quality products of one and the same type is clearly insufficient. This differentiation is lower in the USSR than in other socialist countries. In other words, we sell high-quality goods for relatively lower prices and sell low-quality goods for higher prices compared with their social value. Hence the greater scarcity of high-quality goods, in particular, their classification into a special category, their frequent disappearance from open sale, and their transformation into an object of special distribution, and frequently, into an object of profiteering. Such a pricing practice means redistribution of income in favor of those population strata that have direct or indirect access to scarce high-quality products and that purchase them for a fixed price.

Nor can one ignore the significant fluctuations of retail prices on one and the same commodities that are sold through different channels. In actuality, they attest to the existence of several markets in the nation that differ in assortment, quality, and price of the commodities. In principle, different forms of trade could supplement and reinforce one another and provide better service for the customers. But the fact that different social groups have unequal access to different channels of trade creates a specific form of social inequality, and essentially means the formation of consumer markets in which the ruble has varying purchase power. However, the "equality of all rubles" as the measure of consumption is the basic premise of the wage system. The lack of coordination of these approaches leads to the disruption of socially substantiated proportions of remuneration of differient categories of working people and reduces the effectiveness of the material stimulation of labor.

The third aspect of this problem is associated with drawing the correct boundary between the paid and gratuitous distribution of goods. It must evidently be determined by the socioeconomic functions that are imposed by distribution according to one's labor on the one hand and social consumption funds on the other. Thus, according to one point of view, social consumption funds must guarantee the uniform, socially necessary minimum of such goods as housing, educational and medical services, etc., for all members of society. All such goods that are consumed in excess of the established minimum, on the other hand, must be paid for out of personal income. It would obviously also be possible to propose other criteria for dividing spheres of gratuitous and paid distribution of goods.

In practice, however, such criteria are essentially replaced by physical critieria: some commodities (for example, food, clothing, footwear, tableware, furniture) are sold for money, while others (housing, educational and health care services, etc.) are distributed free of charge or at nominal prices. This practice is associated with serious shortcomings. First of all, it artificially limits the assortment of goods that the population can acquire for the money it earns and therefore lowers the motivation to work intensively and effectively. It is difficult to explain, for example, why a highly skilled, well-paid worker can buy furniture, a refrigerator, and television set, but must wait years to get an apartment to put them in. While it would seem that this contradiction should be resolved by housing construction cooperatives, their existence has only complicated the question even more by making the criterion for distributing goods for a price or free of charge entirely indeterminate.

The distribution of the scarcest goods and services free of charge (and housing and health care services come under just this heading) cannot fail to result in their uneconomical utilization and the artificial intensification of their scarcity. What is more, various kinds of deals— speculation in state housing, the subletting of surplus living accommodations for higher prices, exchange of living accommodations with large cash surcharges, etc.—are frequently concentrated around the distribution of free (and subsidized) goods. The distribution of goods for a price and the unity of prices on similar goods throughout the entire nation are free of such shortcomings.

Finally, sociological research shows that the distribution of goods free of charge from social consumption funds presently favors high- rather than low-income groups. However, one of the most important functions of social funds is to supplement the principle of distribution according to one's labor to a certain degree, to equalize its "injustice" that is imposed on those who despite their desire are not able to work effectively—above all, the sick, the aged, and those who have not reached working age. It seems to us that all this indicates the need to expand the sphere in which services are performed for a fee, including the raising and just differentiation of apartment rents with due regard to the quality and location of the apartments.

All additional payments from the population to the state must without fail be simultaneously returned through appropriate rises in the level of wages, pensions, scholarships, etc. And since this sum will evidently amount to tens of billions of rubles, the reserve concentrated in the state's hands will be sufficient for the dramatic improvement of the wage system.

It is hardly necessary to prove the enormous social significance of these measures—they directly affect the material interests of all social groups. Therefore, there must be careful scientific elaboration of the given problems in their interrelationship in order to consider to the fullest all aspects of social justice and the real interests of the various groups of the population. And the sooner economists, sociologists, and other social scientists start working in this direction, the sooner it will become possible to create conditions for attaining a higher level of socialist justice. The immediate resolution of this complex of problems will be a powerful means of intensifying the human factor, of breaking with adverse trends, and of resolutely accelerating the socioeconomic development of our society.

Notes

1. Here and throughout the article we rely on data from sociological surveys conducted by N. V. Chernina, R. V. Ryvkina, S. Iu. Pavlenko, E. V. Kosals, V. E. Ershova, L. V. Korel', V. S. Tapilina, and V. D. Smirnov, all of whom are affiliated with the Social Problems Section of the Institute of the Economics and Organization of Industrial Production, Siberian Department of the USSR Academy of Sciences, Novosibirsk.

2. Calculated from data presented in *Sotsial'no-psikhologicheskie problemy proizvodstvennogo kollektiva*, Moscow: "Nauka" Publishers, 1983, p. 65.

7 | The Role of Sociology in Accelerating the Development of Soviet Society

The course announced by the Twenty-seventh Congress of the CPSU toward accelerating the economic and social development of our country is becoming more and more a reality. The party is engaged in a titanic effort to eliminate phenomena alien to socialism and to overcome various obstructions on the road to progress: the system of managing the economy is being restructured; the rights of enterprises are being augmented; the barriers to individual and family labor are being eased; the education system is being renovated; an active battle is being waged against unearned income, drunkenness, and crime; an open struggle has been declared against bureaucratism; and some very important changes have affected literature, films, theatre, and other forms of art. But what is most important is that the universal habituation to those half-truths that in a certain sense are worse than lies is resolutely being overcome. We are once again learning to look truth in the eyes, and this fact alone may have the most value.

Not only is the entire system of social relations being restructured in the country, but a heated struggle is going on between the ardent supporters of major changes and those social groups that are ready to do anything to ensure that nothing changes. However, it cannot be otherwise. History shows that no serious social change has ever taken place without an intense struggle between different social forces. As the

"Rol' sotsiologii v uskorenii razvitiia sovetskogo obshchestva," *Sotsiologicheskie issledovaniia*, 1987, no. 2, pp. 3–15. Russian text © 1987 by "Nauka" Publishers, the publishing house of the USSR Academy of Sciences. Translation © 1987 by M. E. Sharpe, Inc. Translated by arrangement with VAAP, the USSR Copyright Agency. Translated by Michel Vale.

restructuring of social relations gathers momentum, the bitterness of this struggle also increases. And this, it seems to me, testifies to the revolutionary character of the changes that are going on. "But," as was observed at the January 1987 Plenum of the Central Committee of the CPSU, "we see that changes for the better take place slowly; restructuring has proven to be more difficult, and the causes of society's problems more profound, than we had previously imagined." Under the new conditions, every work collective and every occupational group must clearly define its place in the restructuring of social relations. This applies to sociologists as well. We must determine which areas in our work are capable of effectively contributing to restructuring, openly discuss the current situation of our science, ascertain the factors that are holding back its development, and develop a system of measures to improve the effectiveness of sociology.

Let us state it bluntly: for a long time the social sciences, far from being in the vanguard, brought up the rear of society. They have lagged behind practice, restricting themselves largely to repetition, explanation, and approval of already-adopted party decisions. This is impossible under the new conditions. Science must not only study the tried and true, but must explore new frontiers, give society ample warning about future difficulties, develop alternative options, and justify the choice of the best decisions. Scientific activity that takes this approach not only can become, but in fact is becoming an active driving force, and an extremely important instrument in restructuring.

But to become such an instrument, the social sciences must first restructure themselves in accordance with the new demands. At a meeting of the chairmen of departments of social sciences, attention was called to the timidity of social thought, the lack of civil courage, and the disinclination of many scientists to study urgent problems. The Central Committee of the party has called on scientists to undertake bold scientific feats and deepen their search, to break with previous stereotypes and dogmas. Whereas several years ago one could only dream of such a state of affairs, today it has become a reality. But can we confidently say which demands of the current period sociology is able to satisfy and which ones it cannot?

New tasks of sociology

The enhanced role of sociology has to do with the fact that every decision affects social interests, changes the situation, and transforms the behavior of a multitude of interacting groups. To develop a strategy for restructuring, administrative organs urgently need complete, accurate, and truthful information about the needs, interests, values, and behavior of social groups in different situations, as well as about the possible influence of this behavior on social processes.

What is needed is further development of the social policy of the party and a clear definition of its specific goals and their interrelationship. The major stages in the realization of the social program must be distinguished, a system of practical measures to implement that program must be developed, and these measures must be differentiated by taking into account the distinctive features of the different regions of the country, as well as of sociodemographic, occupational, sectoral, and other groups.

Sociology should also play an important role in concretizing the party's course toward an acceleration of economic development. Although the general direction of restructuring the management of the economy was clearly defined by the Congress, its practical implementation will require hundreds and thousands of sociologically defined and justified solutions of a more particular nature (for example, what levels of management are superfluous; what types of individual labor activity deserve support and development and what types should be restricted; what differentiation of types of labor should be considered just and what should be considered excessive, etc.). It is necessary to determine the most important interacting groups in the economy as accurately as possible; to study the concrete conditions of their activity, the balance between their rights and duties, the content and methods of realizing interests, the coordination of group interests with social interests, etc. Studies of this group of problems have already yielded noteworthy results.

An equally important task is to supply reliable feedback for the management of restructuring. Indeed, when top-level administrative bodies take a correct and necessary decision, this is only the first, not the last, step on the way toward transforming reality. Later, such a decision will be fleshed out with a multitude of concrete instructions to be interpreted by agencies and local authorities; only then will it change real relations at the local level, either making them more effective or producing negative consequences. Thus it is necessary to maintain a constant sociological monitoring of the course of implementing decisions, and of how the processes of restructuring are progressing in all spheres of public life.

Nor must we forget about an extremely important function of sociology: the cultivation of sociological thinking. Activation of the human factor and overcoming the social apathy of a considerable segment of society, which arose in the previous period, are prime conditions for the success of the transforming activity of the party. We all know how much scientific energy and resources were expended in the search for ways to release atomic energy and put it to peaceful use. The release of man's social energy and its channeling into areas needed by society is a task of equal dimensions and perhaps equal complexity. To achieve this end, sociologists must resolutely develop a social consciousness oriented toward the collective resolution of common problems through our publications in the popular press, and talks on the radio, on television, and in the most varied public forums.

As we see, restructuring is making high and varied demands on sociology. Are we prepared to meet them? This is a serious question requiring a serious answer, i.e., an objective assessment of the contemporary state of sociology in the USSR. Let us then dwell on some of the principal achievements and problems of Soviet sociology.

In the past twenty-five years, Soviet sociology has had definite successes. Its status as an independent science has become more or less established. The Soviet Sociological Association unites about 6,000 individuals and 1.2 thousand group members; the total number of sociologists in the country is 15–20,000. In addition to a specialized sociological institute (Institute of Sociological Research), there are more than forty sociological departments functioning in the USSR Academy of Sciences and the academies of sciences of the union republics. Competent research groups trained in sociology have developed in many social science departments in institutions of higher learning.

The practical returns from research exhibit a definite tendency to increase. Public institutions (soviets, commissions) of sociological research attached to district, municipal, regional, and republic party committees are playing an increasing role in providing information to management. It is estimated that sociological services in industry and other branches of the national economy employ 3–4,000 persons.

The journal *Sociological Research* [Sotsiologicheskie issledovaniia] is now in its thirteenth year, and three years ago the Siberian journal *Economics and Applied Sociology* [Izvestiia SO AN SSSR. Seriia ekonomika i prikladnaia sotsiologiia] was added. The first steps have been taken toward establishing higher sociological education in the country. Fifteen to twenty doctoral and up to fifty candidates' dissertations are defended each year in the area of specialization "applied sociology." The number of publications dealing with sociological topics is increasing constantly.

Major scientific teams have formed and are successfully functioning as "purely" sociological, as well as in socioeconomic, sociodemographic, sociolegal orientations, and are distinguished by a high level of professionalism. They organize their work on the basis of large research projects, make broad use of the systems approach, employ reliable mutually controlling procedures, and take into account worldwide experience in organizing sociological research. But the most important aspect of the activity of these teams is the balance between the theoretical and the empirical in their research, and their thorough and accurate interpretation of their data.

I am referring in particular to recent studies of social indices of development in the USSR, the mode of life of the urban and rural population, and the demographic behavior of the population (Institute of Sociological Research, USSR Academy of Sciences); the problems of social development of the agrarian sector in Siberia, and the social mechanism of economic development of the USSR (Institute of Economics and Organization of Industrial Production, Siberian Section, USSRAcademy of Sciences); socioeconomic issues of well-being (Central Institute of Mathematical Economics, USSR Academy of Sciences); normative aspects of consciousness and behavior in the world of work (Odessa University); ethnosocial problems of the city and countryside (Institute of Ethnography, USSR Academy of Sciences); social problems of economic and state administration (Institute of State and Law, USSR Academy of Sciences). Interesting studies have been carried out in the Institute of the International Labor Movement, USSR Academy of Sciences, the Academy of Social Sciences attached to the Central Committee of the CPSU, the Ufa Aviation Institute, the Perm' Polytechnical Institute, and other institutions of higher learning. The results obtained are actively put to use in elaborating conceptions of the social development of society and of its structural elements.

On the whole Soviet sociology has considerable potential. However, the pace of its development in the past ten to fifteen years has been extremely slow. As a result, sociology is much weaker in the USSR than, say, in Poland or Hungary, or in the developed capitalist countries. Whereas we have only one "purely" sociological journal, in the United States the Sociological Association alone publishes seven such journals, and there are several dozen altogether. While by 1989 we will have graduated our first hundred professional sociologists with a higher education, the 226 sociology departments in the U.S. graduate 6,000 specialists every year, and about 90,000 Americans gain the foundations of sociological knowledge. Whereas specialized courses of study in sociology are given in only a few of our specialized institutions of higher learning, in the U.S. they are given in the absolute majority of higher educational establishments (92 percent). The upshot is that Soviet sociology is considerably behind world standards.

Under conditions of the slow growth of our society, this situation did not bother many people. Moreover, sociologists, who are constantly ferreting out urgent problems, sometimes provoked vexation rather than approval in the administrative apparatus. But the situation has changed. Under the conditions of restructuring the backwardness of sociology has become a brake on the progress of our society. To actively contribute to acceleration, sociology must itself develop at an accelerated pace, both quantitatively and especially qualitatively. But how can this be achieved? We must look into the causes of the situation as it now stands.

First, it must be conceded that the professional level of many sociological studies remains low. Excessive use of descriptive material, an oversimplified treatment of problems, a low level of representativeness of data, mass preparation of plans for social development and reports in a stereotyped manner are by no means rare phenomena. For sociological studies to become a truly efficacious instrument of change, they must be conducted in greater depth, they must be linked with basic theory, and creative inquiry must be intensified. The shift of sociological research teams from a traditional description of the structure and dynamics of the items under study to an elucidation of the social mechanisms of their reproduction is an important step in this direction. Thus, for example, since 1981 the Institute of Economics and Organization of Industrial Production, Siberian Section of the USSR Academy of Sciences, has been studying the social mechanism of development of the economy, consisting of two subsystems: planned state management of the economy and the spontaneous behavior of social groups. In studying the interaction between these subsystems, sociologists endeavor to establish, on the one hand, how group behavior changes in response to the administrative intervention of the state and, on the other, how the economic mechanism of management adapts to the economic behavior of groups. An understanding of the social mechanism, it seems to me, will help to increase the efficacy and concreteness of the recommendations of administrative bodies. Other scholars have had considerable success in studying the social mechanisms of distributive relations, the reproduction of criminality, parasitism, alcoholism etc. This approach makes it possible to direct efforts toward a struggle not against isolated symptoms, but against real problems. However, this approach is not yet well developed. We must also acknowledge the complicity of sociology in the formation of the "half true" view of the problems of our society. Many of the sociological studies carried out in the 1970s and early '80s were unable to avoid varnishing the facts.

Even as they gathered positive facts, some sociologists closed their eyes to increasingly common negative phenomena. In some cases empirical results were adjusted to fit preplanned conclusions. For example, in quite a number of studies of the social structure of Soviet society, one-sided stress was placed on the reduction of interclass and other kinds of social differences, and clearly inadequate attention was devoted to the emergence of new bases of differentiation, linked to shady earnings and to position in the system of political and economic administration.

We expended too little effort on creating a basic sociological theory. The reasons for this are many, but the fact remains. Writers, playwrights, and cinematographers are now presenting works that had been completed in the difficult years but received no understanding at the time. And today these works are extremely necessary to Soviet society. But are there many sociologists who can follow this example? Only a few at best.

We should also reproach ourselves for inadequate civic involvement in the struggle for the institutionalization of sociology. Although we cannot say that the struggle did not take place at all—indeed it was carried on systematically and quite resolutely, otherwise sociology would not have achieved even the little we mentioned earlier—nevertheless, after receiving a few routine refusals we, at least temporarily, accepted the fact that the USSR Ministry of Higher Education did not acknowledge sociology as an independent science, that the departments and agencies to which we sent our scientific reports and recommendations did not always deign to read them, and that the information base of sociology was narrowed, etc.

Finally, we must acknowledge that we did not manifest either the desire or the ability to unite to solve major problems, and to subordinate our personal interests to the public interest. Hostility and misunderstandings among different groups of scholars, and the inability to understand and recognize one another led to the collapse of quite a number of promising sociological teams. All this was compounded by a personnel policy the result of which was to force the most well-known and competent sociologists to leave the Institute of Sociological Research and, more recently, the Institute of Social and Economic Problems, USSR Academy of Sciences, to move to institutions of another specialization, so that they now work practically in solitude at the periphery of sociology. The consequence of this policy was the *de facto* disappearance of the once-famous Leningrad Sociological School and a serious weakening of the staff of the Institute of Sociological Research of the USSR Academy of Sciences, obstructing the successful exercise by this institution of its function as a nationwide theoretical and methodological center for sociological research which it, in principle, ought to have fulfilled.

Thus we certainly have reasons for self-reproach. But if we limit ourselves to acknowledging this, we would be again committing the sin of half-truth. The full truth also requires an examination of the social conditions under which sociology developed in the past fifteen to twenty years and which basically still exist. Let us look into this in more detail.

The status of sociology as a science

The discussion on the subject matter of Marxist-Leninist sociology, which has now gone on for almost two decades, should, it seems to me, be regarded as finished. Most social scientists agree that sociology is a science of the laws of functioning, development, and interaction of social communities of various types. Accordingly, the subject matter of sociology is civil society, which is characterized by a specific social structure, type of family, etc. This definition of the subject matter will enable us, I think, to define quite accurately the place of sociology among the social sciences and, in particular, enable us to distinguish it from scientific communism, which is important for establishing its status. However, the status of sociology as an independent science has not yet been completely acknowledged by everyone. This is evident in facts that may not seem that important, but that, taken together, clearly impede the development of the science.

Here are only a few such facts. Despite the academic tradition of naming institutions in accordance with the names of the corresponding sciences (for example, the Institute of Philosophy, History, Economics, Chemistry, Physics, etc.), the only scientific institution specializing in sociology is called the Institute of "Sociological Research" (evidently in order not to use the word "sociology"). Instead of calling our journal *Problems of Sociology* [Voprosy sotsiologii], by analogy with *Problems of Economics* [Voprosy ekonomiki] or *Problems of Philosophy* [Voprosy filosofii], it is called *Sociological Research* [Sotsiologicheskie issledovaniia].

In our country's system of higher education there is not one sociological faculty, and the departments of sociology can be counted on one's fingers. The lack of a department of sociology in the Academy of Social Sciences attached to the Central Committee of the CPSU is especially alarming. The area of specialization introduced into Moscow State University and Leningrad State University is called not "Sociology" but "Applied Sociology." The area of specialization for the defense of sociological dissertations is given a similar name, as if the theoretical problems of sociology should not be worked on at all.

The list of specialists assigned to work by USSR Gosplan does not contain the area of specialization of sociologists. The role and status of the sociologist in society are also not defined.

We think that all these things are not the result of a confluence of vexatious, random events, but the reflection of a quite conscious denial of the claims of sociology to the status of an independent science. A statement made in the pages of the journal *Vestnik LGU* (1986, no. 2) by Professor V. Ia. El'meev is characteristic in this respect. To the question What is sociology? he answered: This is a generic name for the overall system of social sciences, the most developed of which are historical materialism, political economy, and scientific communism. But sociology does not exist as an independent discipline. And this is the opinion of the head of the department of applied sociology, one of three such departments in the country. Sociology was again treated as a particular philosophical discipline, but not as an independent science, in the proceedings of the recent conference of heads of departments of social sciences.

It is necessary to consistently institutionalize sociology as a science with an independent and extremely topical subject matter, to clearly determine its role and place in the resolution of the concrete tasks of accelerating growth, and to create the conditions for its own development. The status of sociologists in society, in enterprises, and in organizations must be defined. The renaming of the Institute for Sociological

Research to the Institute of Sociology, and the periodical *Sociological Research* to *Problems of Sociology*, and the area of specialization in the higher academic courses now entitled "Applied Sociology" to "Sociology," could be of fundamental significance. Moreover, this area of specialization should be removed from under the umbrella of philosophy and economics, and scholars should be granted degrees directly in the sociological sciences. Sociology should be included along with the history of the CPSU, political economy, historical materialism, and scientific communism as one of those fundamental philosophical disciplines in which the teaching burden is reduced to a lower level in connection with the increased volume of out-of-classroom educative work.

The attitude to sociology as a science can and must be fundamentally changed at the highest party and state levels.

Equipping sociology with competent personnel

The skilled personnel situation is best reflected by the formula "sociology without sociologists." Since an education in sociology does not exist in our country, even our leading specialists are, strictly speaking, self-taught. To be sure, the old generation of scholars which has now been working for a quarter of a century has accumulated considerable knowledge and could quite effectively convey it to the next generation. However, most often such "transmissions" take place either within sociological teams of scholars or through postgraduate and field work. In either case, the product is "piecework," whereas mass training of sociologists has never existed and does not exist now. The departments of applied sociology opened in 1984 at Moscow State University and Leningrad State University are small, and attract almost no professional sociologists as teachers. The quality of cadres thus trained is therefore dubious. Instruction in sociological disciplines in institutes of advanced training, universities of Marxism-Leninism, and departments of social science professions is thus slow and difficult. The "vacuum" of professionals trained in sociology is filled by nonspecialists, which lowers the level of sociological research and compromises the science. To overcome this abnormal situation, promoted by the conservative position adopted by the USSR Ministry of Higher Education, it is necessary to develop, establish, and carry out an integral program of development of education of sociology. This program could include:

1. The establishment of faculties and departments of sociology in universities in cities where professional sociological teams exist that are capable of teaching at a sufficiently high level. These cities include Gor'kii, Kuibyshev, Novosibirsk, Minsk, Odessa, Perm', Sverdlovsk, and a number of others.

2. The opening of departments in "applied sociology" or "economic sociology" in leading colleges specializing in economics, and in the economic faculties of the large specialized (i.e., technical, agricultural, commercial, etc.) institutions of higher learning. As teaching cadres are formed, specialized courses in sociology and social psychology designed for all students can be introduced into the curricula of these institutions.

3. The creation of a consistent system of retraining and advanced training of sociologists who do not have an education in sociology in the faculties of the social science professions, in universities of Marxism-Leninism, in institutions for advanced training, and other types of establishments to meet existing and future cadre needs of the agencies of social development.

4. The expansion of the system of sociological education for workers in party, soviet, and economic agencies, for managers and leading specialists in enterprises, as well as for the staff of Komsomol and trade union organizations by the higher party school, the special faculties, municipal sociological seminars, etc.

5. Increasing the publication of academic, methodological, and popular sociological literature oriented toward different forms of education and self-education and diverse categories of students.

The status of social statistics

Studies in which theoretical hypotheses are verified constitute only a small portion of the information about the social life of society. The most important sources here are state social statistics, which are intended to systematically portray the course of demographic, economic, and social processes. The availability of a developed set of social statistics, including surveys of public opinion, enable scientists to concentrate on the solution of the most complex questions. In turn, they can provide active procedural and methodological help in developing social statistics.

In the majority of developed countries social statistics provide a firm basis for sociological research. Their data are widely published and have a considerable ideological role. For example, the government of Japan annually publishes the report "On the Life of the Nation," an elaborate set of social statistics, in a large edition. In addition to an empirical analysis of the social situation in the year covered by the report, time series for many indices over the past ten to fifteen years are also given, and the statistical data in each section of the report are necessarily compared with the results of questionnaires of the population.

Among socialist countries, Hungary may have the most developed social statistics. Regular sociological-statistical studies, based on a nationwide sample and embracing a broad range of problems, are supplemented by almost two dozen panel studies providing for the long-run observation of the destinies of various groups of the population (young families, graduates of certain institutions of higher learning, etc.). After the data have been processed the statistical authorities pass them on to scholars.

In the USSR the situation is different. In this respect we tend to bring up the rear among the developed countries. I should stipulate that from my point of view social statistics are not what lies in the storerooms of the Central Statistical Administration, but the final results of data processing published in the public press and accessible to a broad range of people.

A few years ago Japanese scholars with a loyal attitude to our country asked me why the USSR did not have social statistics. Observing that the Japanese literature contained many fabrications about the social development of the USSR, they complained that they couldn't find any materials necessary to refute this misinformation. Sociologists from other countries have expressed similar considerations. But most importantly, social statistics are extremely necessary for our own purposes.

Social statistics were in fact never completely restored after the sad memories of the '30s. In the '60s and '70s some positive tendencies appeared, but soon the development of social statistics suffered a reversal. Thus, publication of materials from national population censuses became increasingly meager (and even almost disappeared!), and all new areas of social information were sealed off.

We have become accustomed to the fact that data on the prevalence of criminality, the frequency of suicides, the alcohol consumption rate, the consumption of narcotics, and the ecological situation in various cities and districts are not published, although all these phenomena are traditional subject matter for statistics in economically developed countries. But how can we explain the lack of information in the press about the migration between regions, between cities and the country-side? Why are data about the structure of the morbidity of the population concealed? Why is information about the differentiation in the level and structure of incomes, and the general well-being of the population so meager? Even if negative tendencies had emerged in these areas, wouldn't it have been more correct to call them to the attention of the public, to discuss ways of dealing with the problem jointly? The course toward a restructuring of the system of social relations presented by the Twenty-seventh Congress of the CPSU provides for just such an approach.

For the sake of objectivity we must say that the gathering and analysis of social information has increased considerably lately. However, it has become more difficult for scientific organizations to obtain data from the Central Statistical Administration because of a multitude of refined bureaucratic hitches. In particular, Siberian scholars often simply "yield their position" and renounce further efforts, since it proves impossible to obtain information during the time allotted for trips to Moscow. But it is of fundamental importance, and an essential ingredient of the openness of social life, that the data of social statistics should be accessible not only to scholars, but also to broad strata of the population. If information about the conditions of their own life activity (e.g., the extent of environmental pollution, the level of industrial accidents, the crime rate, etc.) is concealed from people, more active involvement in production or in the political spheres can hardly be expected from them. People's trust and support can be obtained only in return for placing trust in them. As M. S. Gorbachev said, "Without openness there can be no democracy, no mass political creativity or participation in management. This is the guarantee of the state's attitude, pervaded by a sense of responsibility, to the affairs of tens of millions of workers, collective farmers, intellectuals, and the starting point for the psychological restructuring of our cadres."[1]

The lack of social statistics forces teams of sociologists to gather not only in-depth information, but even the simplest sociodemographic information on the composition of the population, the territorial distribution of the elements of the social and cultural infrastructure, the incomes and well-being of different social groups, etc. But scientific investigations cannot and should not compete with state statistics in representativeness, the scope of the problems studied, the regularity of data gathered, or the comparability of the results. Moreover, shifting the tasks of the Central Statistical Administration onto research teams limits the latter's ability to exercise their strictly scientific functions.

Let me note that the new leadership established in the USSR Central Statistical Administration has already begun to have a beneficial influence on relations in science. As a result of a detailed discussion of the problem with the departments of economics of the USSR Academy of Sciences, the Central Statistical Administration has decided to facilitate economists' use of statistical information. This decision should be extended to teams of sociologists working in the Department of Philosophy and Law, USSR Academy of Sciences. But the main point is that the creation of useful social statistics—an important precondition for increasing the active social involvement of Soviet people—should be accelerated.

Links with practice; adoption of the results of research

Since one of the functions of sociology is to provide scientific material to management, most sociological studies are oriented towards "assisting practice." However, the real participation of sociologists in managerial activity is not great, and frankly it is difficult to name one major managerial decision touching upon the fundamental interests of many social strata and groups that was based on a prior reliable and representative sociological investigation. On the other hand, examples to the contrary are plentiful. Let me just mention the unfounded line adopted in the early '60s to eliminate private plots; the massive transformation of collective farms into state farms, which undermined profit-and-loss accounting in agriculture; the classification of rural localities into those with prospects and those without, which resulted in a distortion in the network of settlements in many rural areas of the country; the mass construction of multistoried buildings in rural localities, the inhabitants of which are longing to return to their own houses; the abolition of small rural schools, which resulted in a forced efflux of the population into cities, etc.

As a rule, state expert evaluations of vast projects (e.g., the diverting of the Siberian and northern rivers into the southern regions of the country, or reclaiming the territory of the Baikal–Amur railway) are accomplished with minimal or no participation of sociologists. Sociologists are inadequately consulted in planning, setting up, verifying, and assessing results of socioeconomic experiments. This stems from the fact that management's need for a sociological basis to decisions is undefined, and most of those for whom sociological information would be useful are not prepared to receive it. The predominance of a technocratic over a social public consciousness is also at fault. It is no accident that some sociological recommendations proposed ten to twenty years ago are just beginning to be used now.

To all this it must be added that sociology often is forced to rest content with a monologue instead of a dialogue with the administrative bodies. Often, we do not receive a response to reports sent to state organizations, we do not know how the material we presented has been assessed or used, whether our recommendations have been accepted, what problems should be further studied, etc.

The absence of a working dialogue between sociology and administrative practice harms both sides. Sociology moves away from practice against its will, does not develop the skills of dealing with complex social problems, and becomes speculative if not scholastic. This further diminishes its prestige in the eyes of managerial cadres, makes people reluctant to use its services, and often leads to socially unsound management.

It seems to me that this situation must be rectified from both ends at the same time. On the one hand, sociologists must increase the efficacy, reliability, and real administrative orientation of their recommendations so that these recommendations contain not only answers to the question of what must be done, but also by whom and how it must be done, as well as what would be the probable consequences of the social solutions proposed.

On the other hand, administrative workers should pay more heed to sociology, without which not one serious social problem can be solved nowadays. Further, the legal status of sociology in its relations with administration must be clearly defined, sociologists must be adequately represented in state evaluating committees of USSR Gosplan and the Gosplans of the union republics, and their participation in socioeconomic experiments must be strengthened.

The possibility of actively involving sociology in the practical process of restructuring of society is also limited, it seems to me, by the inadequate specialization of teams of sociologists, and the limited division of labor among them. Thus academic science, which plays the role of the ''shaft horse'' in the sociological team, must deal with theoretical, methodological, and procedural problems at the same time, while sociology in higher education must train a workforce of specialists. For both, studies of a managerial and administrative orientation are only one of the aspects of scientific activity. This means that it is necessary to develop at an accelerated pace those areas of sociology that specialize directly in social monitoring of the implementation of administrative decisions. These areas can be created only within administrative bodies themselves. We are speaking of applied sociological services attached to party, soviet, and Komsomol bodies, sectoral agencies, production associations, and enterprises. Let us look into this in more detail.

The development of applied sociology

Although applied sociological services first began to be established more than ten years ago, they have not yet developed very extensively. There are about a thousand such units in the whole country. The vast majority of applied sociological services are concentrated in industry, with much fewer of them in construction and only a few in the system of party, Komsomol, and soviet administration, and attached to territorial administrative bodies and cultural institutions. Roughly speaking, fewer than 2 percent of industrial enterprises have such services, and in one-third of these the entire service is represented by one worker, by two or three workers in another third, by four to seven in 20 percent, and by eight or more workers in only 13–14 percent.

We may adduce the following main reasons for the slow development of applied sociology. First, there is the very minor role played by social indices in the system for evaluating the activity of enterprises and their managers, the lack of real responsibility of enterprises to state, party, and trade union bodies for the resolution of social questions. Further, there is the low level of professional training of applied sociologists, only 5 percent of whom have had even a minimum sociological training, including training in the universities of Marxism-Leninism. Finally, there is the low level of development of the methodology of applied sociology, the focus of which should be not so much investigatory as analytic, planning, and implementing activity; the poor methodological and technical equipment of applied sociological services has made for an obsession with questionnaires. More than 70 percent of the procedures are developed independently by each service by poorly trained cadres.

As we know, in April 1986 the USSR Council of Ministers' State Committee on Labor and Wages, the USSR Academy of Sciences, and the All-Union Central Council of Trade Unions adopted a resolution on "Improving the Organization of Sociological Work in the Branches of the National Economy,"[2] aimed at a fundamental improvement in the work of applied sociological services. The document ratified a model statute for services for the social development of an enterprise (organization, or ministry). As regards how the Soviet Sociological Association can assist these services, I would mention the following as indispensable steps.

First: increased attention to the methodology of sociology; development of a general schema for such work, and creation of a set of standardized procedures for all areas of applied sociological service activity.

Second: collection, generalization, perfection, and publication by the Soviet Sociological Association of procedures and other materials that shed light on the progressive experience of the work of applied sociological services. It would be useful for this purpose to conduct a nationwide competitive review of the work of applied sociological services in the next year or two. We should also think about the creation of a financially self-sufficient center for applied sociology, with informational, methodological, and teaching functions, and extensive duplicating equipment, within the system of the USSR Council of Ministers' State Committee on Labor and Wages or attached to the Soviet Sociological Association.

Third: certification of cadres working in applied sociological services, with the issuance of individual qualification certificates, and later mandatory attendance by all workers in these services at a centralized system for advanced training (which must still be created), and the organization of apprenticeships for applied sociological service workers in the leading sociological organizations of the country.

These and other ways to accelerate the development of applied sociology require collective discussion and practical implementation.

The limitations on the objects suitable for sociological investigation and possibilities for publishing the results of such research

Earlier I spoke about the important political role played by an open discussion of acute social problems. Often such problems take on the features of permanent "syndromes," making it necessary to penetrate to the roots of such phenomena, and to attempt a thorough theoretical interpretation and explanation of them. But this is impossible without a free and objective discussion of complex nontraditional questions. It is this to which the Central Committee of the party is directing our attention. More than once at the Congress, and after it, the extreme damage done by the existence of areas and groups ''beyond criticism'' was pointed out. I should think that the preservation of any zones and groups ''outside the complex of sociological investigations'' is no less harmful.

Society is an integral system and hence ''pain'' at one of its points is often caused by processes taking place at completely different points. To treat the body correctly we must know how it functions. But sociologists, who have raised some burning questions in their investigations and have attempted to deal with complex problems, until recently have too often encountered, and indeed encounter even today, the inscription ''access prohibited to outsiders.''

I personally have had occasion to encounter restrictions with regard to both the subjects of a scheduled survey and the content of the problem studied. There were periods when it was perhaps easier to enumerate what was permissible for discussion in the scientific literature than what was prohibited. Let me speak bluntly: If these limitations are maintained, one cannot seriously expect effective recommendations from science. To obtain the full measure of what science has to offer, it is necessary not only to permit, but also to welcome, encourage, and commission studies of the most painful and acute questions requiring immediate and prompt solution. The light of sociological research must penetrate into the remotest corners of social life, expose the rubbish that has accumulated, and encourage a prompt and total housecleaning in the home in which we all live.

As regards the publication of sociological investigations, the attitude of the central and local publishing houses has for a long time been more than cautious. Moreover, in the last ten to fifteen years the number of publishing houses putting out sociological literature was considerably constricted. The number of institutions with the right to publish works in sociology has been reduced to an even greater extent. In contrast to institutes in the natural sciences, institutes specializing in the social sciences have no right to publish monographs independently. The size of collections of scientific studies released for publication is limited to ten printed sheets. The number of articles in which an author, including a group leader, may participate is strictly limited and the size of each article is also restricted; the functions of author and editor must not be combined. On the whole, the publication of the results of sociological studies is hampered by so many bureaucratic rules that often three to four years pass between the moment a manuscript is ready and the time it is finally published. Under conditions of accelerated development of society, during this time not only empirical data but scientific findings may become obsolete. In any case, the rapid enrichment of public awareness with new social facts and ideas is out of the question.

We may add to all this that the majority of sociological monographs and collections are published in small editions. This is due partly to the fact that many of them have only a speciously scientific character, and are nonproblematic, nonjournalistic, and uninteresting to the general reader. Instead of arousing thought, these works curiously exult over everything being just fine. Sometimes it is said that they are "fulfilling a propaganda function." But it is obvious that today such "propaganda" not only does not achieve its objectives, but even does serious harm. It does not mobilize people to deal with problems, but rather develops in them a psychology of dependence, an attitude that a rising standard of living and improvement in living conditions are guaranteed by a progressive social system and do not depend on their personal efforts. An embellished description of the state of affairs in this or that district, city, or branch of the economy simply increases the dissatisfaction of those who do not see such "successes" in their own surroundings. In exactly the same way, excessively optimistic forecasts of the further development of the country (region, city, or enterprise) create unfounded expectations, and ultimately disappointment.

We must expand the educative influence of sociological literature on broad strata of the population. Materials and conclusions from completed studies must be brought to the working masses through newspapers, popular periodicals, radio, television, pamphlets from the "Znanie" Society, the materials of TASS, and the Academy of Pedagogical Sciences. This is also one of the conditions for transforming our science into a first-hand tool of restructuring.

The implementation of the proposed measures for stimulating and accelerating the development of sociology will require time and quite an effort. It is naive to think that there will be no difficulties. But these difficulties cannot be compared with the gain that will accrue to the country once sociology attains a higher qualitative level.

Notes

1. *Materialy XXVII s"ezda KPSS.* Moscow: Politizdat, 1986, p. 60.
2. *Sotsiologicheskie issledovaniia*, 1986, no. 3, pp. 88–95.

8 | Urgent Problems in the Theory of Economic Sociology

The Twenty-seventh Congress of the CPSU, the resolution of the Central Committee of the CPSU on the work of the periodical *Kommunist*, and the All-Union Conference of Heads of Departments of the Social Sciences have all stressed the necessity of taking a new look at some of the cardinal problems of social development and overcoming dogmatism and narrowmindedness in the way they are conceived.[1] One scientific domain whose timeliness is growing is economic sociology—a science that studies social structure and the social mechanisms of development of the society's economy.

The crucial conditions for accelerating social development are activation of the human factor, fuller and more effective use of the individual's labor and intellectual potential, and reawakening the creative energy of the masses and channeling it into the mainstream of social interests. But how can we achieve every person's identification with the goals of society and involvement in the process of restructuring? The economic behavior of groups is, of course, dependent primarily on their interests, which are determined by their objective position in the structure of society. This means that the human factor will be activated not so much by words as by a well-directed and forceful socioeconomic policy that will ensure the integration of personal and group (collective) interests with the interests of society. To provide a scientific foundation for the shaping of such a policy, to contribute to its develop-

"Aktual'nye problemy ekonomiko-sotsiologicheskoi teorii," *Izvestiia Sibirskogo otdeleniia akademii nauk SSSR, Seriia ekonomika i prikladnoi sotsiologii*, no. 13, issue 3, September 1987, pp. 3–14. Russian text © 1987 by "Nauka" Publishers, the publishing house of the USSR Academy of Sciences. Translation © 1988 by M. E. Sharpe, Inc. Translated by arrangement with VAAP, the USSR Copyright Agency. Translated by Michel Vale.

ment, and to scientifically monitor its practical implementation are tasks of utmost importance for economic sociology.

Like most sciences, economic sociology fulfills theoretical, fact-finding, and applied functions. Its theoretical functions involve discovering objective laws of interaction between the economic and social spheres of society, and developing a methodology for studying social structures and the mechanisms and regulators of economic processes.

The fact-finding functions of this science consist in the study of such concrete and real entities as the socioeconomic structure of society; the position, interests, behavior, and interaction of classes, strata, and groups in the economic sphere; the specific social mechanisms of different economic processes; public opinion on questions of socioeconomic development, etc. On the one hand, these functions help society know itself as a body social (by familiarizing the masses of workers with the results of sociological investigations), and on the other hand ensure feedback for social management (by acquainting the cadres of party, state, and economic leadership with these results).

The applied functions of economic sociology consist in directly providing scientific underpinnings to the processes of decision making in the management of the socioeconomic development of the country, its republics, regions, cities, districts, as well as the branches of the economy, associations, and enterprises. In contrast to scientific fact-finding investigations, applied studies are oriented toward discovering how effective management of a particular object is, whether the required unity of personal, collective, and social interests is being achieved, and whether the modes of people's economic behavior conditioned by the existing system of management are rational and effective. A knowledge of these circumstances makes it possible to develop recommendations for improving the management of social development.

These theoretical, fact-finding, and applied functions of economic sociology, far from excluding one another, even mutually stimulate one another. Thus accelerated development of theory heightens the need for scientific empirical research to verify hypotheses. This empirical research becomes more purposeful and effective in the process. The development of such research not only provides an information base for the further progress of theory, but it also helps to detect the "burning points" in social life, and direct the attention of administrative bodies to acute socioeconomic problems. Finally, applied research, which is related to direct participation in management, draws the attention of scholars to urgent questions of practice, and prevents drifting into scholastic arguments or "knowledge for the sake of knowing." Consequently, for a relatively mature science, a balanced development of theoretical, empirical, and applied investigations is most effective.

But when a new science is in the process of development, it is theory that plays the pioneering role, inasmuch as it opens the way to empirical and applied research. This is also true of economic sociology, which is still in its early stages in the USSR. The first task of this new area of science is to provide a foundation for its initial theoretical and methodological conception. The following features are characteristic of its present state:

1. The unresolved nature of a number of urgent problems of theory, owing to the fact that until recently the possibility of creative development of theory in social sciences was generally quite limited. Attempts to revise theoretical dogmas and bring theory into line with practice encountered a very guarded attitude and were sometimes even labeled political mistakes.

2. The negative influence of "traditional" social science theory on the development of empirical research within the compass of economic sociology. The fact is that some "theoreticians," accustomed to passing off wishes for reality, would orient the concrete sociological studies carried out under their direction for the most part toward confirming predetermined results, e.g., "proving" that the boundaries between all social strata and groups were being obliterated, that the society was moving toward complete social homogeneity, that there were no conflicts between nations and nationalities, that a fundamentally new type of person was developing who invariably subordinated his own personal or collective interests to social interests, etc. An objective analysis of socioeconomic phenomena and processes in the country was considered by these scholars to be a conscious denigration of reality. This situation substantially delayed the formation of an objective scientific picture of contemporary Soviet society.

3. The feeble development of the applied aspect of economic sociology. Although most studies in this sphere culminate with recommendations to administrative bodies, the studies themselves do not yet come close to sufficiently serving the needs of restructuring. This may be attributed to a certain inertia on the part of scientists accustomed to less rigorous empirical research, and to the inability and sometimes the unwillingness of administrative personnel to formulate precisely what they want of the science or to use the results of investigations undertaken on personal initiative.

In the light of what we have said it is important, first, to accelerate the development of theory in economic sociology, subordinating a substantive treatment of its problems to the urgent tasks of restructuring economic relations; second, to strengthen the relationship between theoretical and empirical investigations, and not to permit a gap between theoretical developments and the study of actual reality; third, to concretize substantially the recommendations submitted to administrative bodies, and to give them a realistic and practical character. The starting point for this set of tasks is to develop theory in economic sociology. We may accordingly distinguish four groups of problems whose development is particularly urgent:

1. The development of a systemic conception of the structure of society from the standpoint of economic sociology, the structure that predetermines the interests, behavior, and interaction among the various elements of society in the economic sphere.

2. The study of the social mechanisms of economic processes, of the restructuring of social relations, and of changes in the social qualities of the human factor in the economy.

3. The determination of the economic-sociological properties whose acquisition will signify the transition of Soviet society to a higher stage of socialism.

4. Providing a scientific grounding for the social strategy of restructuring of societal relations, the acceleration of socioeconomic development, and the transition to a qualitatively new stage of society.

Let us now examine what these four groups of problems consist of concretely.

Political economy views society as a system of interacting classes occupying different places in the system of social production. In addition it sometimes distinguishes intraclass strata differing substantially in the complexity of the labor they perform. The merits of political economy's conception of the social structure of society are its simplicity, its visibility, and its wholeness. But it is insufficient for the practical needs of managing socioeconomic processes. That requires knowledge of more concrete strata and groups that represent economic interests and are the subject of economic relations. The aggregate of such interrelated groups is the structure of society seen from the standpoint of economic sociology, the economic-sociological structure of society.

Analysis shows that the subjects of some types of production relations are ethnodemographic groups, others are socioterritorial groups, others are organizational and departmental groups, a fourth category includes occupational and official status groups, still others are familial and household groups, and a sixth group are the work collectives of organizations. The total number of typological groups distinguishable in terms of these criteria amounts to several hundred, and indeed it is these groups that are the real subjects of economic relations and economic development.

The economic-sociological structure of society is a constantly self-reproducing system of relations between groups occupying different positions in the structure of management of the economy and society, in different situations relative to social property, and differing in the content and conditions of their labor, the extent to which they have access to the social infrastructure, in the level and sources of their personal incomes, the extent of their accumulated family possessions, the orientation of their economic interests, and the type of behavior in the economic sphere.

To study the structure of society as defined by economic sociology entails:

—determining the social groups forming it, their position, their interests, and their behavior in the nation's economy;

—constructing a composite and noncontradictory description of the social interaction of these groups that would ensure the functioning of the social economy and the achievement of long-term social goals;

—describing societal (social, economic, and political) institutions responsible for the reproduction and development of the qualitative attributes of the economic-sociological structure of society.

Today sociologists study comparatively discrete areas of economic relations, e.g., the sociological aspects of planning, the sociology of the collective or family contract, socioeconomic interactions and the attitude of hierarchical groups of administrative personnel to restructuring, the socioterritorial structure of different regions, the income differentiation and well-being of sociodemographic groups of families, etc. The study of the economic-sociological structure of society is a new, fundamentally more complicated scientific task. Moreover, there is a great theoretical and practical need for defining this task and dealing with it.

A second group of problems has to do with studying the social mechanisms of economic development, which includes changes in the economic-sociological structure of society.

Let us assume that we have already studied how this structure is set up and how it functions. Is this knowledge sufficient for managing the development of the economy? Evidently not. A ship that has embarked upon a journey must take into account not only the speed of its own movement, but also the strength of ocean currents. The development of society also has its own uncontrollable endogenous components. This is evident from the simple fact that in the absence of planned control from the state and party, the economic-sociological structure of society does not remain as it is but gradually changes on the basis of its own internal laws of development. The development of this structure can be consciously steered only if these laws are known. To speak figuratively, the task is not to start up a car that is standing still and steer it in the necessary direction, but to redirect a car that is already moving, ensuring that it is progressing to a goal. This can be done only if we know where the car is going, at what speed, and why. In our case this means that it is necessary to study the objective mechanisms of development of the socioeconomic sphere. If we know the structure and principles of action of these mechanisms we can attempt to "readjust" them in such a way that the real economic-sociological structure of society will be brought more rapidly and more deliberately closer to the next stage of socialism.

There are also more practical considerations bearing out the necessity of studying the social mechanisms of economic development. Indeed, every year economists and sociologists send administrative bodies a multitude of proposals on how to improve the management of the economy. But the great bulk of these proposals remain unrealized, and the effectiveness of those that are usually leaves much to be desired. One of the reasons for this is that the recommendations are more often formulated in terms of goals that must be achieved rather than in terms of the means to achieve these goals. For example, it is proposed that the wages of workers be brought more closely into correspondence with the amount and quality of labor expended, that workers' participation in management be intensified, that a "sense of being the owner" of social property should be cultivated in them, that the possibilities enjoyed by some groups of the population to extract unearned income be blocked, etc. How to do this is left to the managerial and administrative personnel themselves. But to reorganize the economic-sociological structure of society without attacking the mechanisms reproducing it is as ineffective as burning a field and leaving the roots of weeds in the ground.

It is no accident that the interest of social scientists in the social mechanisms of the processes they study has increased in recent years.[2] But the study of these mechanisms is still in its early stages and leaves ample room for posing new tasks.

A third group of problems has to do with developing an economic-sociological conception of the essential features of the stage of socialism into which Soviet society will be passing in the coming decades. A thorough grounding of this conception will provide stable theoretical underpinnings to a strategy for managing the development of society and will make it possible to define its long-term goals in more concrete and clear-cut terms.

As we know, the goals of economic and social development of socialism, though closely interconnected, are in an ambiguous relation to one another. In particular, under conditions of slow development and a low level of efficiency of production, economic goals to a certain extent have primacy over social goals. Social policy in such a situation is aimed first and foremost at stimulating the members of society to perform more actively in the economy and only secondarily toward overcoming socially unjustified inequalities in their positions.

But the subordination of social goals to economic goals is justified only for short periods of time, limited to one or two five-year periods. Over the longer term, the principal goal of the development of socialism becomes the creation of a more progressive system of social relations that will ensure the all-round development of the individual, the realization of personal aptitudes, and the remuneration of representatives of all social groups in accordance with work performed. This long-term goal is purely social in nature and the effective development of the economy becomes the means for achieving it.

What we have said has a direct bearing on the tasks of preparing the theoretical foundation for the next stage of the development of socialism. The program of the CPSU contains benchmarks for describing its essential features. These are: first, theoretically justifying the necessity of the transition of Soviet society to a qualitatively new stage of development through a deep and radical restructuring of the entire system of existing social relations; second, the formulation of the principal goals of the party's economic strategy and social policy; third, an extensive characterization of the social, economic, and political advantages of developed socialism compared with capitalism. These theses combined basically reflect the present level of development of Soviet social science, but they do not justify regarding the problem of the long-term goals of development of our society as solved. In reality this problem requires deep theoretical study.

Let us take the formulation of the goals of the party's social policy as an example. The first of these is referred to in the CPSU program as the steady improvement of the conditions of life and work of Soviet people. This goal is most timely, since the material level of many social groups is still low, and working conditions in a number of branches and occupations remain harsh, harmful, and dangerous to health. However, attempts to extrapolate the probable transformation of this goal as socialism develops further encounter deficiencies in the development of various aspects of theory. For example, the question arises whether the material consumption of society should increase indefinitely or whether there is a rational limit to this growth. Can one speak of an optimal (for each period of time) level of material consumption sufficient for satisfying rational needs that at the same time would not place too great a burden on the environment? And if it makes sense to pose the question in this way, how should relations of distribution and consumption of material goods change as we approach the "optimal" level? What changes will this bring in the organization of production, the balance between working time and leisure time, the lifestyle of the population, etc.? These questions are being widely discussed in the Soviet scientific literature, but a consensus has not yet emerged.

The second goal of social policy is an increasingly complete implementation of the principle of social justice in all spheres of social relations. The advancement of this goal elicited a broad response among working people and received general acclaim. But the theoretical content of such concepts as social justice in general and socialist justice in particular are as yet inadequately grounded. It is no accident that there is no section in the CPSU program that explores the concrete content of this goal, although each of the other three goals has a section of its own devoted to it. Social scientists must work out sound concrete criteria of justice in economic, social, legal, and political relations, and reveal the relationship between the principles of socialist justice on the one hand and social equality on the other.

I have often expressed my opinion in the press that the economic-sociological aspect of the concept of "socialist justice" basically involves a consistent fulfillment of the principle "from each according to his abilities, to each according to his work." This, in turn, presupposes:

—gradually reducing differences in the "starting conditions" of personal development and the occupational and skill growth of members of all social groups;

—orienting personnel policy toward a fuller and more objective consideration of the practical and personal qualities of workers when promoting them to positions requiring complicated creative labor, and especially to positions involving personnel management;

—providing all groups of workers with the possibility of full self-fulfillment in work and creative activity, in social production and outside of it;

—strengthening the dependence of personal income on the results of the labor of individual workers and work collectives, and eradicating all forms of unearned income;

—creating a uniform consumer goods market for all groups of the population, equalizing the buying power of the ruble territorially and socially, overcoming the socially unjustified deviation of prices from the social cost of consumer goods;

—ensuring a socially justified distribution of the costs of maintaining the disabled segment of the population between their families and the state.

Of course there are other views of the content of the concept of "social justice," which means that a deeper theoretical grounding and discussion of it are necessary.

It is also necessary to bear in mind that even a broad scientific discussion of this problem in the best of cases will help disclose only the "objective" aspect of social justice, i.e., the extent to which the real system of social relations corresponds to the theoretical model of socialism. But for the successful development of society and the further sociopolitical integration of its groups, the "subjective" aspect of justice, i.e., what the bulk of working people perceive to be just social relations, is no less, if not even more, important. People's subjective assessment of the justice of any social phenomenon depends first and foremost on its real characteristics. But there are no automatic connections here, since individual groups' conceptions of justice are very different and usually are "colored" by their own interests. It is impossible to reduce these notions to one common "denominator" since they often have opposing contents.

Clearly the ideas of mass strata and groups such as workers, collective farmers, and engineering and technical personnel are the most significant for social development. Changes in the public opinion of these groups could in principle serve as a criterion of the real movement of society toward greater justice or injustice. But at present a large proportion of workers are inclined to identify social justice with social equality. Hence, they recognize a relatively equal distribution as just, but a wide differentiation of income owing to substantial differences in work is regarded as unjust. This indicates the necessity not only of thorough studies of the opinions of social groups on social justice, but also the deliberate cultivation among working people of correct notions of justice.

The third goal of social policy formulated in the CPSU program is the further convergence of social classes, strata, and groups, and the overcoming of substantial differences between mental and physical work, and between city and countryside. These tasks are quite timely, and the basic paths for dealing with them are clear. But there are also quite a number of unresolved theoretical problems in this area. First, the real movement of society in these directions is slow, and in certain periods inconsistent. This requires a study and perhaps an adjustment of the mechanisms of these processes.

Second, even as differences inherited from the past are being overcome, new social differences are being formed in society that are not always subjected to scientific analysis. These include social differences between hierarchical groups of managerial personnel, between workers in "rich" and "poor" departments, between branches of material production and the nonproductive sphere, between inhabitants of small and large cities, between the working population and pensioners, etc. To develop a long-term social strategy economic sociology must more accurately and thoroughly define the essence of such concepts as social differentiation, social homogeneity, essential social differences, etc.

A fourth group of problems has to do with the social strategy of restructuring of social relations, including economic relations. Such a strategy is necessary because the economic mechanism of managing the economy is intimately connected with the social structure of society, so that any change in this mechanism affects the position of social groups. The restructuring of economic relations does not take place in a vacuum, but in a domain where the vital interests of people intersect. As M. S. Gorbachev pointed out in his speech at the Eighteenth Conference of Trade Unions of the USSR, "Restructuring is now affecting everyone: members of the Politburo, secretaries of the Central Committee, members of the government, workers, collective farmers, and the intelligentsia. The whole of society is affected. It is affecting the interest of each and everyone."[3] Members of social groups whose position is improved as a result of the transformations in progress endeavor to assist restructuring, while groups whose interests are suffering resist it. If the specific features of the economic, social, and official positions of various categories of workers are known, their actual attitude to restructuring can be forecast with sufficient probability.

The transformation of economic relations influences the situation of social groups, first, through the expected result, and second, through the process of restructuring itself. This transformation is of course aimed at expanding the economic independence and responsibility of work collectives, developing self-management in production, encouraging initiative in economic management and in production, developing the cooperative movement, expanding the sphere of individual work activity, and, on this basis, achieving a more rapid growth in the well-being of the population than in earlier years. These changes will mainly help to improve the position of the most competent (skilled, energetic, and enterprising) segment of the population, while people with limited capacities, a low level of skill, and poor health will be in a less favorable position. The transfer of many rights from the upper levels of economic management to lower levels should inevitably lead to a reduction in the total number of cadres in ministries and departments, and this will mean the transfer of some personnel from administration to the sphere of production, which will hardly please any of them. Finally, the transformation of economic relations is not at all advantageous to the corrupt segment of managerial cadres who have acted (and perhaps are still acting) in alliance with operators in the "shadow" economy: restructuring threatens both with their demise. Herein perhaps lies the roots of the events in Alma Ata in December 1986: reactionary forces do not yield ground without a struggle.

Recently quite a number of attempts have been undertaken to portray the deployment of social forces around restructuring,[4] but most of them have been more in the nature of hypotheses than the results of special sociological studies.[5] Such studies, it must be said, encounter methodological difficulties since one cannot expect negative responses to direct questions about people's attitude to restructuring. But this problem is not unique. It is also encountered by sociologists who have studied unearned income, alcoholism and drunkenness, and other forms of deviant behavior. Nonetheless, scientists are developing methods that will enable them to overcome such difficulties. The study of the interests and behavior of groups with regard to the transformation of social relations is necessary both for testing initial hypotheses about the forces abetting or obstructing restructuring, as well as for obtaining more concrete notions about the number, qualitative composition, and position of the groups involved and the ways they go about realizing their interests.

So far we have discussed the influence that the expected results of restructuring may have on the behavior of social groups. But it also influences people's position, seen as a process developing over time. The fact is that the stability of social relations and the reliability of forms of social life have an independent value for a considerable number of people. Many people object to the destruction of traditional relations for the purpose of replacing them with unaccustomed ones. The adjustment of new social relations requires time, during which old problems often become more acute, new problems arise, and confidence in the future diminishes. The results of trial and error, which are essential to restructuring, influence the lives of many social groups, but this influence is especially strong on workers in the state administration and those responsible for managing the economy. For most of them, things are becoming more difficult than before. It is therefore important to ensure that the scheduling and duration of these transformations are correct.

A reform may be either rapid and radical or protracted and gradual. The first type, the swift implementation of a radical reform of social relations, contains the danger of political adventurism, manifested in an isolation of practical restructuring from its "scientific rearguard." There is also the danger of a bureaucratization of restructuring, i.e., the supplanting of genuine transforming activity by a pseudo-activity aimed at fulfilling "handed-down" indicators. The experience of the mass diffusion of the collective contract has provided many examples of this type. Despite its outward paradox, the bureaucratization of the process of democratization of management is a real danger, whose inevitable consequence will be to compromise the fundamental ideas of restructuring.

But to procrastinate with restructuring involves dangers that are just as great. Thus, judging from the experience of the reform in the '80s in Hungary, the gradual introduction of isolated changes in the economic mechanism over time was unable to bring about a qualitative change in the system of economic management. Moreover, the slow development of the reform reduces the stability of social life and causes growing discontent among the population. Under certain conditions this creates the necessity not only of temporary retreats, but also a protracted renunciation of further implementation of the reform, which is in contradiction with the fundamental interests of society.

The optimal strategy of restructuring, it would seem, would be first a sound and thorough scientific analysis of its fundamental issues, the development of a firmly grounded conception embracing all basic elements of the reform, and second, relatively rapid implementation (over one or two years) of a comprehensive transformation of the system of economic relations. But these ideas are no more than a hypothesis. The actual choice of a concrete strategy of social restructuring by the political leaders of the country presupposes not only the prior resolution of a number of theoretical problems, but also the need to conduct methodologically sound economic-sociological studies of the position, interests, opinions, and behavior of representative social groups.

The above list of problems is very broad and is addressed not only to economic sociology, but to a number of other sciences as well. Moreover, studies in economic sociology, having received a certain impetus, generate new areas of science and affect new collectives as they develop. Under these circumstances the section on social problems of the Institute of Economics and Organization of Industrial Production of the Siberian Section, USSR Academy of Sciences, which has taken the initiative in developing economic sociology in the USSR, must narrow its area of investigation and pose more circumscribed but clearly defined tasks that are within its capacities.

In 1986–90, our scientific collective will be devoting most of its attention to the study of some of the most important aspects of the social mechanism of development of the economy. Developments of an analytic nature will for the time being predominate over investigations aimed at generalization, since the structure of the subject matter is extremely complex. In addition to continuing the comprehensive study of the specific social mechanism of development of the agrarian sector in the Altai region, the Siberian Section will be working on two theoretical themes of economic sociology: "Social regulators of the socialist economy and ways to improve their effectiveness," and "Mechanisms of managing the social development of territorial systems and production organizations." The author of the present article, together with R. V. Ryvkina, is in charge of the first topic, whose essence is as follows.

The initial conception of those working on the topic of social regulators of the economy is shown in the diagram. To explain it we can start with the unit "The economic mechanism of management of the economy." By this mechanism is meant the aggregate of normative and legal relations regulating the organization, planning, and stimulation of various types of economic activity.[6]

The economic mechanism is subject to the influence of the social and political institutions that evolve over time in every society, including norms and rules of behavior fixed in social traditions, national culture, and customs. The considerable role of social institutions in economic development is confirmed by such phenomena as the arbitrary administrative supervision of production activity, which often takes place contrary to the requirements of the economic mechanism, or the "shadow" and semilegal economy, which "gets around" this mechanism from another direction.

Of course the social norms of economic activity are not separated from formal legal norms by an "iron wall." With time, shadow and semilegal relations may turn into legal forms and become elements of the formal mechanism of economic management. Such, for example, are the relations of the family contract, the work of freelance construction brigades in the countryside, and certain other relations (see the chart, connection 1).

The interaction between the economic mechanism and social and political institutions forms the social mechanism of management of the economy, i.e., an integral system of written and unwritten but quite widespread norms and rules of work and economic activity, some set down in law, and some not, all determining the interests and modes of behavior of social groups in the economic sphere (connections 2 and 3).

Socioeconomic behavior reflects the subjective aspect of activity, which is conditioned by group interests and reflects people's personal relation to its goals, conditions, and methods, and exerts a substantial influence on its effectiveness. People's economic behavior depends not only on the social mechanism of management of the economy (connection 4), but also on the position of social groups in the economic-sociological structure (connection 5). This structure is closely linked to the economic mechanism of management of the economy (connection 6) as well as with social and political institutions (connection 7). The difference is that the restructuring of the economic mechanism is the

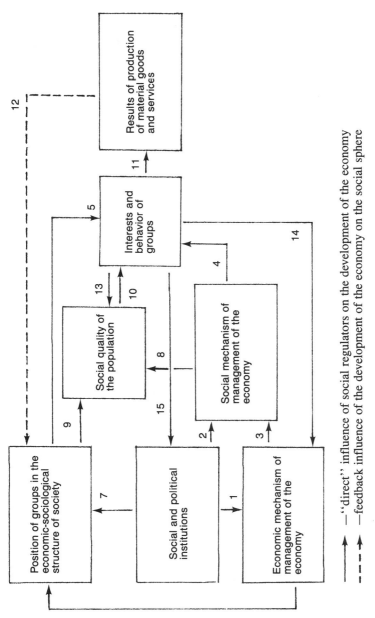

Basic Conception of the System of Social Regulators of the Economy

— "direct" influence of social regulators on the development of the economy

- - - — feedback influence of the development of the economy on the social sphere

result of the professional activity of managerial and administrative personnel, and hence it is relatively mobile and flexible. Social and political institutions are more resistant to change but are, to a certain extent, manageable and controllable, as evidenced by, for instance, the successful struggle against the deeply rooted practice of excessive consumption of alcohol. As regards the economic-sociological structure, it reflects the integral results of the development of social relations over a long period of time and hence is especially sluggish. Managing changes in it can be implemented only indirectly, mainly through the economic mechanism, but also to a lesser extent through sociopolitical institutions.

The economic-sociological structure of society determines the balance between personal, collective, and social interests. The more rigorously the principle of socialist justice is observed in all spheres of social life, the more thorough the integration of group and social interests, and the more actively involved is people's economic behavior. Violations of socialist justice, on the other hand, lead to alienation of the individual from social interests, and encourage various forms of deviant behavior.

The social mechanism of management and the economic-sociological structure of society influence the interests and behavior of people both directly and indirectly—through the social quality of the population (connections 8, 9, and 10). By this term, the quality of the population, we mean the totality of characteristics on which constructive (work, intellectual, creative) potential depends, and on the other hand the characteristics of the population's normative consciousness (the system of value orientations, needs, and preferences). The social qualities of a population include their state of physical and mental health, the level of education and culture, the occupation and skill structure, the degree of discipline and responsibility, the degree of development of a legal awareness, morality and ethics, personal merit and merit on the job, etc.

A social quality is a stable characteristic of large groups of people, the main features of which are passed on from generation to generation. But this quality gradually changes under the influence of the social mechanism of management, which actively molds a specific normative consciousness, and of the economic-sociological structure, which predetermines the possibilities of social and cultural development of social groups (connections 8 and 9).

The interests and behavior of people are represented by a single common unit on the diagram, although in reality they have a complex heterogeneous structure. From the standpoint of our projected study, we may distinguish three types of results of economic-sociological behavior: (a) the production of material goods and services, (b) the production of the person himself, and (c) the development of social relations. The results of behavior and activity in the first sphere acquire a material form that is alienated from the subjects. A generalized expression of these results are, first, the dimensions and qualitative structure of the social product, the national income, and the accumulation and consumption funds (connection 11); and second, changes in the well-being of different social groups (connection 12). The results of the second and third types of activity and behavior are manifested in changes in the social quality of the population (connection 13), in the improvement of the economic mechanism (connection 14), and in social and political institutions (connection 15).

Such is the initial theoretical conception of our research team on social regulators of a socialist economy. It will be developed and refined as empirical research progresses. But even now this conception is being used as a methodological means for implementing a clear division of labor among members of the research team. The results of this research may very well prove to be interesting both theoretically and practically.

Notes

1. Information on the session of the Scientific Council of the Institute of Economics and Organization of Industrial Production, Siberian Section, USSR Academy of Sciences, devoted to research and economic sociology is found in the article by V. I. Fedoseev in the present issue of this journal [*Izvestiia Sibirskogo otdeleniia akademii nauk SSSR, Seriia ekonomika i prikladnoi sotsiologii*, no. 13, issue 3, September 1987].

2. On this matter see R. V. Ryvkina and L. Ia. Kosals, "Rol' sotsial'nykh mekhanizmov v uskorenii sotsial'no-ekonomicheskogo razvitiia obshchestva," *Izvestiia SO AN SSSR, Ser. ekonomiki i prikladnoi sotsiologii*, 1986, no. 12, pp. 4–5.

3. M. S. Gorbachev, "Perestroika—krovnoe delo naroda: Rech' na XVII s"ezde profsoiuzov SSSR," *Pravda*, February 26, 1987.

4. See G. Kh. Popov, "Perestroika v ekonomike," *Pravda*, January 22, 1987.

5. E. G. Iasin, R. V. Ryvkina, A. V. Petrikov, and other scholars have studied the attitudes of particular social groups to various aspects of restructuring.

6. See A. M. Rumiantsev, "O sovershenstvovanii ekonomicheskogo mekhanizma upravleniia proizvodstvom," *Voprosy ekonomiki*, 1975, no. 11, pp. 3–4; V. Senchagov, "Razvitie sotsialisticheskogo khoziaistvennogo mekhanizma," ibid., 1978, no. 5.

INTERVIEW | **Restructuring Corresponds to the Strategic Interests of the Majority**

Q. At serious turning points in life a person usually thinks back on the past and tries to interpret the present, as it were, rising above everyday matters. Probably the same thing also happens in society. We are today living through precisely such a moment: we are at the crossroads of the historical fate of society. Right now many people are asking: Who are we? Where are we going? The opinions of social scientists are naturally primary here. . . .

As the saying goes: ask me something easier. . . . You are asking me as a social scientist, right? Unfortunately, science is not yet ready to answer this kind of question. After all, it is not yet clear just what restructuring really means.

After the June Plenum of the Central Committee of the party, we can speak more definitely about the directions of economic transformation, but after all, they do not exhaust restructuring: that much is obvious. New social processes have begun in all spheres of life. Perhaps some of them will enter into contradiction with others? We don't know. Science must now have at its disposal at least two models—one for the transitional period, and one for the ideal state toward which society is to move. But, as far as I know, they aren't available.

"Perestroika sootvetstvuet strategicheskim interesam bol'shinstva," *Znanie–sila*, 1987, No. 11, pp. 29–31, 34–38. Russian text © 1987 by "Znanie–sila," published by the All-Union "Knowledge" Society of the USSR. Translation © 1988 by M. E. Sharpe, Inc. Translated by arrangement with VAAP, the USSR Copyright Agency. Translated by Stephen P. Dunn.

Q. Is this a reproach to social scientists, including yourself?

Yes and no. It is our custom to scold social scientists in all kinds of situations. But does the problem lie only in the social scientists, their sluggishness, their lack of inquisitiveness? Who is to blame for the fact that we have arrived at the present revolutionary changes with such a weak social science theory? We mustn't forget that for a long time there was no demand for such theory on the part of society, and the management agencies didn't need it. Any attempt to develop the theory, to depart from dogmas that were fossilized in quotations was at best received with caution, and more frequently was evaluated as a political mistake—and this, you know, was fraught with very unpleasant consequences. I'm not even talking about the 1930s and 1940s, but this was the case until very recently.

To a large extent our social sciences are oriented to administration. This is the case not only in that obviously opportunistic sense which involves the linking of the theoretical positions that are generally accepted at any given moment to every pronouncement "from above." And not only in the equally opportunistic concrete studies with results given in advance: if we know that the homogeneity of society "must" increase, then such studies inevitably find an erasure of the dividing lines between workers and peasants, between the city and the countryside, between mental and physical labor, although the ordinary eye, not equipped with a theory, easily discovers the opposite.

I'm now talking about something else—the fact that honest scientists, not out of fear or selfish motives, but out of the best intentions, are often prepared to respond to the request or order of the administration to provide it immediately with scientific recommendations about some matter—including advice on problems that haven't been specially studied. These recommendations, based not on theory but rather on "common sense," tell the administration very little that is new, and rather provoke disappointments with science.

Naturally, science is not only not forbidden to serve the needs of practice, but that is one of its main functions. However, it is only one. . . . There is also the value of theory in and of itself, the value of the scientific acquisition of knowledge. And there is also one other function, that of promoting the self-knowledge of society. Unfortunately, our science has for a long time hardly worked on these goals, and has finally lived long enough to hear the reproach uttered from the highest tribune that we don't know the society we live in.

Q. It is clear how the internal logic of research brought you from the study of concrete social problems to the creation of economic sociology. But in working out your conception of the economic-sociological structure of society, didn't you rely on definite theoretical principles and premises, and on a tradition?

Certainly. My collaborator, Doctor of Economic Sciences R. V. Ryvkina, and I have tried to use all of the considerable "stock" that was created by Soviet and foreign Marxist scholars. Of course, we also turned to Marx and Lenin. The powerful methodology they created works excellently when applied to our society today.

For example, one of the central concepts of Marxism is ownership of the means of production. In the course on political economy a detailed analysis is given of private ownership of the means of production and its social consequences under capitalism: the fact that poverty and wealth live side by side, hired labor, economically determined inequality of political and social rights. But when one passes over to the description of socialism in terms of political economy, with its public ownership of the means of production, then man with his interests and activity disappears, and the exposition is transformed into a scholastic exercise, into abstract formulae, which there's no way of connecting with the real life around us. That was how it was when I was a student, and that's how it still is.

But the concept of ownership of the means of production retains its explanatory force for the description of our society at all stages of its development. Property that has been socialized is placed at the disposal of the state. I'm not a historian, but I think that the state has never possessed under any other socioeconomic order simultaneously such political, economic, and military power. This gives the state an exceptional opportunity to implement a goal-oriented program for the development of society. But this is also fraught with great dangers: bureaucratism, the scale of which is inversely proportional to the degree of democracy in the political, public, and economic life of the country, and the huge risk connected with each incorrect decision of the center, or merely a decision that is not taken in a timely manner. Lenin more than once warned of these dangers. He spoke of the close similarity between socialism and state capitalism, the "watershed" between which is determined only by what happens to the surplus product,— whether it goes to enrich individual ruling groups or to satisfy the needs of all members of society and to solve social problems. That is, the difference lies only in one step, in one question: in whose hands does power rest? Besides, that step, as Lenin wrote, can in principle be taken in both directions.

The attitude toward work and its results, the active involvement of people in public affairs, depend to a large degree on the forms in which social property is implemented, on the degree to which it is actually social, compared to the degree to which it is simply state property: on how large the groups are that have the opportunity to control it in practice. This is one of the most important characteristics that determine the position of a group in society. Thus, the specific relationship to the means of production and to social property can be used to explain not only the status of a minister, but also the particular position of an equipment operator in the countryside, of the driver of a state-owned car, and of a worker in trade.

The principles advanced by Lenin for determining the social-class structure of society also work quite well today. He relied on three main characteristics: relationship to the means of production, role in the social organization of labor, size of the consumed share of social wealth and the means by which it is received. Different combinations of the values of these characteristics determine the socioeconomic position of each social group, its interests, and its behavior in interaction with other groups.

Q. In your conception, the economy, and indeed the whole life of society, appears as a field of interaction of group interests. It is clear that these interests determine the attitude toward restructuring. But in general, sociology, which was only reborn at the beginning of the 1960s after an imposed lethargy, began immediately to talk about the interests of employees as something deserving of the most concentrated study. In the beginning, what was at issue were simple things, which were clear to everyone: you can't make people stay in the countryside or at an enterprise if you don't show concern for them; the development of a public and consumer-service infrastructure of production is obligatory for the development of production itself.

The next step was taken by economists in the discussions preceding the reform in the mid–1960s. The main task of the 1965 reform was declared by economists to be the reconciling of the interests of the individual employee, the enterprise, and the economy as a whole. To this day we are trying to solve this task, and this is what the latest party documents are directed toward. Can it be said that you are developing

*the ideas of those years in your latest works—and that the current
economic policy retains continuity with these ideas?*

There's no question but that there is some continuity. But over the
intervening years there has taken place what I consider to be an extremely important change in the concept of the role of human beings in
the economy and the life of society. I have in mind the replacement of
the concept of "labor resources" by the concept of "the human factor."

The goal of our society has for many years been formulated in the
following way: to create conditions for the harmonious development of
the human being and for the satisfaction of his or her constantly
increasing needs. But for a long time it was somehow an abstraction
that could only be approached after creating the necessary material-
technical base. And until that time the population of the country remains primarily a "labor resource" of the economy, as it were, in the
same category as technical, raw-material, and power resources.

The concept of "labor resources" is an economic one, by means of
which it is convenient to study the processes of formation, distribution,
redistribution, and use of the work force. This is what economists have
done, and are doing to this day. But whether we like it or not, a certain
image of the employee as a passive object of management stands behind
this concept. After all, resources cannot formulate their own goals, do
not have personal interests, do not manifest initiative, and in general do
not act in a goal-directed way. They are formed, distributed, and used
by someone else on the basis of societal interests that are external to
them.

We have to be concerned with the preservation and reproduction of
resources. The essence of social tasks can be understood precisely in
this way: we must first of all provide working people with a normal
wage and the necessary minimum of goods and services. Isn't this
necessary? To this day there are shortages of housing, foodstuffs, child-
care facilities, and the like. To this day the ministries and agencies
make all kinds of cuts in investments in "social, cultural, and consumer
services," using this means to mend the holes in production and to put
up new plants on empty land. This was what the sociologists of the early
1960s were chiefly struggling against, arguing that people would not
work well as long as they lived badly.

But who said that a "well-fed," more or less well-provided-for
person will automatically give his or her all on the job, and will manage

the public's property with initiative and in a conscientious way? But we need precisely this kind of attitude toward the job from working people today. After all, no "resource"—neither nature nor equipment—will ensure, in and of itself, the intensive development of the economy.

The need for an autonomous worker has called forth the new concept of the "human factor." The word "factor" means the cause or moving force of something, and this means that the accent now falls on the active, moving role of man in the economy. The new concept, laid down in many party documents, which is already in great vogue, has in essence crowded out "labor resources." It is true that behind this concept we do not see the idea of man as the goal of production (a factor is something auxiliary, necessary for something else), but behind it we no longer see the concept of man as a passive object of management. This is a huge step forward, a new stage in the development of social consciousness and of society itself.

Q. Did the approach to man as a labor resource, and to social and economic life as processes that could be completely managed, correspond to the degree of development of society at the previous stage?

No, such a primitive model never reflected reality. I have said that it is suitable only for narrow, empirical economic calculations, but by no means as a "philosophy of management." Man is by nature active and has always been so. The social structure of our society during the whole period of its existence has been and remains considerably more complex than the traditional model of "workers–peasants–intelligentsia." And there has always been a struggle of group interests.

Q. But still, the previous conception of "labor resources" worked, and management was efficient enough to provide for industrialization and to win a very difficult war. Restructuring became necessary when the old method had exhausted its possibilities. . . .

Our history should hardly be described only as forward movement along a straight line. If too high a price is paid for efficiency, it is already not efficient enough. What about the "costs" of collectivization? What about the mass repressions? Who can show that this was an inescapable price paid for efficiency? On the other hand, it is very easy to demonstrate that this was to the advantage of particular social groups, and that they actively implemented their narrow interests—at the expense of the interests of the main part of society. Any shortage is to someone's advantage, whether it is a shortage of rights, information, openness, goods, or services.

Q. Aren't you placing too much emphasis on the improvement of the relationships of distribution? We should first enlarge the "societal pie," and then each person's share would be bigger.

You make "relationships of distribution" sound very material. . . .

There are two approaches to the place of distribution in the life of society—a narrower and a broader one. The first goes according to the widely popular model, "production–distribution–exchange–consumption." The other—and the one I like better—assumes that distribution takes place at every stage of reproduction; that is, it constitutes a necessary part of production, and exchange, and consumption. At the stage of production, for example, means of production, jobs, professional rights and obligations, work orders, and wages are distributed. You see, groups are constantly dividing something among themselves, and not only the position of each of them, but in the final analysis the size of the "societal pie," as you expressed it, depends on the results of this procedure.

It is no accident that passions flare up around relationships of distribution. By working conscientiously, and thereby increasing the national income, and with it the fund of public consumption, we can increase the welfare of the group, but at the cost of a great deal of labor and very gradually, a little at a time. On the other hand, by redistributing what has already been created, we can increase the well-being of certain groups by a factor of two or three or ten, and very fast in the bargain. Of course—here you are right—without increasing the size of the "common pie," this can only be done at the expense of other groups.

Q. But will that really happen?!

What do you mean: "will it happen?" Hasn't it been happening all along, and isn't it still happening? Research shows the existence of a considerable number of groups with unjustifiably high incomes. And haven't you yourself encountered this? When you are shortchanged in the store, or when you buy something at a speculative price, this is also redistribution of income.

As for "what will happen," I think that a well-developed social democracy will give social groups the opportunity to limit each other's appetites.

You studied child psychology, right? How does the child learn to live among his peers? At first, everyone in the group wants to play the role of Little Red Riding Hood, and no one wants the role of the Wolf; no one wants to go around looking, and everyone wants to hide. Later, children begin to understand that things can't be done that way or there will be no games, and so they somehow agree among themselves. Forming of lines, casting of lots, counting-out rhymes—all these are the first principles of socially literate distribution. This is also the basis of socialization—when children work out these rules for themselves, arriving at the inevitable thought of limiting their demands.

Something like this also happens in society. All over the world there exists what is called group egoism, and if it is not limited by anything—if there is no control on the part of other groups—its consequences can be terrifying. A typical example is the Mafia. Democracy, in the final analysis, is only the right of each social group to express, defend and implement its own interests. It is not a confection which always has to be sweet and good tasting.

The main "rule of the game" in the life of socialist society must be the principle of social justice. Concepts of justice differ, and they are always colored by group interests, but they still have a healthy common foundation. It is unjust to receive what you haven't earned, because it was certainly taken away from someone else. It is unjust to "reap the rent" from fertile land, when the same amount is paid for the harvest taken from the black-earth region and from the harvest grown on the poor lands of the Pskov area. It is unjust when some people make decisions, and other people suffer the consequences if they turn out to be incorrect.

Q. But are you sure that in the free play of interest, it is precisely these just principles that will be worked out? So far, forces that are not particularly to our liking—nationalism, speculating on the general concern for the safety of cultural monuments, or for the severe consequences of alcoholism, and so forth—are putting themselves forward quite actively. . . .

Yes: all this is not very pleasant. But is it so bad that such moods, enthusiasms, and groups declare themselves openly? We have seen them and understood them, and does society really have nothing to set up against them? Without openness and democracy all this would continue to exist, but it would be driven inside and concealed.

But why have you mentioned this and not, for example, the history of the plan to redirect the northern and Siberian rivers? This is a most striking example of how public opinion stood up to bureaucratic interests—and won. Previously it was a good deal more passive. In the face of an extremely severe housing shortage, palaces were built in the cities, and natural resources were barbarously plundered—and behind each such action stood somebody's interests, which were implemented essentially without control, and with no limitation whatever. As Pushkin has it, "the people remained silent." And now, finally, they are beginning, slowly and awkwardly, to speak of their interests, their demands, and to express their opinions. When they begin to speak louder, the bureaucrats' armchairs will tremble. . . .

You must understand that the constant interaction of social groups and the contradictory nature of their interests are not something thought up by sociologists: these relationships cannot be "abolished." You can ignore them; you can try to confine them within the framework of petty regulations, but this, as we know from experience, is fraught with considerably more serious violations of social justice.

It seems to me that the real problem right now is not the "excess" of democracy, but our lack of skill in living with it. A certain degree of social development and social culture is needed and so far we do not particularly shine in this area.

In order to become a real force for development and restructuring, interests have to at least be brought to consciousness. Sociological studies show that even this initial process is going rather slowly. Do you want a paradox? You know who is most satisfied with the level of public services in the countryside? From our data it is the inhabitants of the most underdeveloped settlements which do not even have stores or elementary schools. Or—from a quite different "opera" (your own journal recently wrote about this): factory directors would like to buy freely the raw materials, subsidiary materials, machines, and spare parts that they need for production; they are opposed to the distribution of resources "by rationing." But they would like to retain the compulsory distribution of their own production "by a rationing," in order to guarantee its sale. It seems clear that these are elements of different economic systems which do not match each other—but no, they coexist peacefully in the same heads. Can you effectively defend your own interests if you do not clearly know what they consist of? After all, directors today are one of the most active groups in society. . . .

Q. Perhaps those who answered the questionnaire did not particularly believe in the seriousness of the changes and wanted to take advantage of the moment by "begging" for something in the usual way? It seems to me that grown-up people have a pretty good idea of what they would like.

I'm not sure. You may be right about tactical interests, but not strategic ones.

A tactical interest is specific and immediate. But a strategic interest consists in providing for the long-term possibility of realizing one's interests. Do you remember how Lenin struggled against the "economists," reproaching them with the fact that, in struggling for the "worker's kopeck," they neglected something considerably more important: political—that is, strategic interests?

It seems obvious: enterprises should be given more independence since factory directors and collective farm chairmen are bound hand and foot by petty regulations. Do you think that they see in their sleep how to achieve this independence? We thought so too when we began our study, but then we became convinced that this was not entirely the case. The primary problem for them is the supply of materials and equipment and not economic rights. Here you have a typical case of tactical interests taking precedence over strategic ones.

Q. We are contemporaries of historic events affecting the fate of the country—not only contemporaries, but also participants. Each person has to choose, and each choice will change something important, by no means only in his or her personal biography. How can we avoid being mistaken, and do this correctly? To what degree has the history of the preceding decades and the present condition of society prepared us for this?

Look: in order to work out a sociopolitical strategy, you have to know the disposition of forces clearly, see the interacting groups in society, and understand their interests. We do not know the society in which we live. This is a reproach not only for scientists, but it applies to each citizen of the country. The self-consciousness of our society is not yet all that highly developed.

In the 1930s the heightened, politicized self-consciousness of the citizens of the first socialist republic in the world was severely deformed. The same slogans with which the people at one time had undertaken the October Revolution and which had gained for the land of the soviets the sympathy of many progressive people in the world continued to be heard. The power of socialist ideas made people capable of heroism on the job and gave them hope and patience. But at the same time there was an effort to inculcate a highly specific concept of the social structure of society: a chieftain who was concerned about everybody and thought about everybody (and for everybody); his "sons and daughters," who inhabited a fortunate country and were boundlessly grateful to him for the right to inhabit it; small but sinister groups of "enemies," "revisionists," "wreckers," originating from who knows where, spoiling produce, poisoning the wells, ruining the harvest, and the struggle required concentrated vigilance on everybody's part.

The power of the ideology of that time was nourished by at least two sources: the power of socialist ideas, which no one disavowed, and fear, because the correspondence of thoughts and even feelings with the models offered was almost a condition of survival.

The consciousness of society was in part suppressed (quite often physically), and in part put to sleep. Coming out of the movie theatre, setting aside the newspaper, or turning off the radio a person saw around him or her something very different from what he or she had just been shown or told—but this was here, in this particular place, and there where the movie was shot, everything was probably different, and someday it would be that way here as well. . . . Of course, there was a secret feeling of reality, but it could not become a social force precisely because it was secret.

Social psychology teaches us that the picture of the world and the social position held by each person is developed in small, so-called "primary" groups—in the family, in the company of close friends. The fear of repressions destroyed mutual confidence, without which these groups cannot exist. This fear was quite well-founded. I remember that as late as the mid 1950s we—that is, several young Communists at the Institute of Economics of the USSR Academy of Sciences—decided to write a letter to someone in authority in regard to some event that had upset us (I no longer remember what it was). We wrote the letter and sought the advice of a scientific supervisor, who liked me. When he looked at the letter he turned downright pale, tore it up, and said:

"Have you lost your minds? This is a 'collective,' 'group action!' " In the mid 1930s he had been 35 years old and knew quite well what was what.

Social themes were either avoided or dealt with according to the clichés current at the moment. In addition, to be split up like this is unpleasant for a normal person who wants to be at one with everyone and wants to believe. So people put themselves to sleep. And as for what went on in the heads of the peasants during collectivization, we can learn about this now, if at all, only from the most recent belles-lettres.

Q. But you said yourself that man is always active.

I was talking about a different kind of activism! Each person tried to realize his or her own "tactical interest" to the extent possible. The collective-farm woman, by hook and by crook, pushed her daughter Valia into the city where she would have a better, easier life, and more to eat, but she didn't think about the interests of all peasant children, of her social group as a whole. In the cities, people were fighting for a bigger room, but very few discussed the housing problem as such, especially since it was far from safe.

Q. It seems to me that we took the largest step toward self-consciousness in 1956. The Twentieth Congress of the party has already been felt by several generations to be a major event not only in the history of society but literally in the personal biographies of an enormous number of people—we can say virtually all. All of us are in some sense children of 1956. And now, 30 years later, we face the same problem and the same need to understand who we are, where we have come from, and where we are going.

Certainly, the Twentieth Congress was a signal for awakening—although I think that for older people the signals began to sound quite a bit earlier, even before Stalin's death. Just remember the famous "case of the doctors," and the wave of anti-Semitism that accompanied it. What decent person could believe all that? Then came the exposure of Beria. They said the usual: not enough enemies had been killed off in 1937. But questions arose: how could the genius of all ages and peoples not have seen an enemy alongside him? Perhaps it was then, for the first time, that we began to look into the faces of the leaders of the country.

Stalin was at an unattainable height; he was not discussed, but worshipped. However the people began to see that those who took his place were human beings.

In 1956 I was 29 years old. The Twentieth Congress confirmed my deepest doubts as to the correctness of what was happening in the country. Along with my generation I took it as a piece of good fortune, a liberation, a cleansing. But for those who were a generation or two older, it was much more difficult to fully accept the revelations of the Twentieth Congress. This meant, after all, to review almost your entire former life, and to recognize that you share responsibility. Administrative posts, even down to the least important, continued for a long time to be occupied by people of that generation, "the accomplices." They could not, did not want to, and were unable to act in any other way. Besides, who said that there was "another way?" The socioeconomic structures remained essentially what they had been, centralization was not weakened, and as before, people were told one thing but saw something else around them. It is true that those who had undergone repression returned—those that survived—and that, if you like, is one of the major achievements of 1956.

People began to live better, and were no longer held captive by the constant need to strive for the most elementary of things. The level of education rose. Demands increased. But the turn toward real democratization of the management of the economy and of public life did not take place. It was difficult to implement the appeals to become master of the production process and to take an active position in society. The necessary economic and social mechanisms for this had not been worked out. The activism of young people in the 1960s now and again encountered resistance and changed the direction of many people. I think that in the so-called period of stagnation, activism, generally speaking, was not weakened, but rather increased, except that it was directed only partially to what were declared to be public goals, and to a considerable degree away from these goals. Some people put special effort into furnishing a newly-acquired house; others wrote "for the drawer" without expecting to be published; still others, taking advantage of the relaxed controls and increasing disorder swiped something for their family nests.

There were also, as there always have been, those who, in spite of everything, tried to implement their right to work in a more rational and sensible way, and in the common interest. Sometimes they were supported, and attempts were made to disseminate progressive experience.

But in the course of being disseminated this experience, as a rule, was emasculated when it came into conflict with the traditional relationships of production. Most often, it immediately encountered sharp opposition from the bureaucracy, and it is no accident that Ivan Khudenko, the true founder of the contract system in agriculture, died in prison, and that this was written about in the press for the first time quite recently.

The center was no longer in command of the economic situation but did not want to let go of its own command methods of management. The reform of 1965 was choked by paper and by contradictory instructions. The condition of the economy deteriorated, but everyone, as usual, pretended that the opposite was happening. The country had long since stopped living within its means, and this, as we know, cannot go on indefinitely.

Q. But now no one pretends any longer—open up any newspaper!

Yes, thanks to the efforts of your journalistic colleagues the society has come to know itself considerably better. Newspapers are grabbed up right away and the lament of many people is: "I don't have time to read everything." Each one is touched by his or her own thing—one person by the unusual truth about the condition of the economy instead of the customary fanfares; another by the Rostov affair, which showed the true face and power of corruption. I am not even talking about such things as the film "Repentance," and the novel *Children of the Arbat*, which have overturned the consciousness of many. We seem literally to have taken a new look at our history, both ancient and recent, and I think that the active part of society has increasingly acknowledged the impossibility of living in the old way.

A ship is saved not merely by those who have an incentive to do so—they may be asleep in their bunks—but by those among them who are aware of the danger. Thus, if we consider openness an inseparable part of restructuring (and I'm quite sure about this), then it has already begun to form the social base for a new course of development.

But, while recognizing that restructuring corresponds to the strategic interests of the majority, we still have to learn democracy, and rational management of the economy, and finally we simply have to learn to work. Many people have become quite unaccustomed to this. The elections for directors which have been held in some places have shown that we do not have a good command of elementary democratic procedures.

We have to learn to defend our interests. Who, for example, has more reason to be concerned about the protection of the environment than local inhabitants? And who has less reason than the agents and ministries of water management, the chemical industry, the forest industry, and others? Yet the game is still played all the time "into one goal": the air, the water, the earth is polluted; all kinds of "maximum permissible concentrations" of harmful substances are exceeded, and the inhabitants do nothing but write letters—sometimes indignant, and sometimes expressing suffering, to the center. This is essentially what they can do in their attempt to defend their right to live under healthy conditions.

The inhabitants of cities and villages in essence do not control their representatives in the local organs, and this is what has made possible the well-known sad stories in Uzbekistan and in Krasnodar Territory, the leaders of which not only ignored the interests of working people, but openly acted against them. Territorial groups rarely turn out to be capable of independent activism. It is possible, for example, to pay no attention to the abandoned lots around apartment buildings, and to write complaints and demands that trees and bushes be planted—and it is also possible to put everything in order with your own hands and to plant your own trees and bushes. You will agree that the latter mode of action is not all that widespread.

Q. To be honest, I also skip past the vacant lots under the windows and try not to look at them. We live, basically, either behind the closed doors of our apartments or at our places of work. Still, you would agree that the success of restructuring depends more on our work than on the planting of trees and shrubs. . . .

Moderate your sarcasm on this score. The point at issue is not decorative plantings, but our capacity for initiative and our readiness to defend and implement our interests. Only if we learn this can restructuring become irreversible. In addition, the cultural level manifests itself in everything: the cleanliness of streets; the naturalness of democratic procedures; the habit of self-organization; and the fact of being accustomed, let us say, to a certain level of services. One thing does not determine the other, but they are interconnected. . . .

Q. But still, who, right now, in your opinion, supports restructuring?

Are you asking me as a sociologist? Then I will tell you honestly that I do not know. I will be able to answer when technically reliable and representative surveys have been conducted, and these have only begun. But restructuring doesn't have to be "supported" as though it were being done by someone else, from outside, and all of us must amiably give our unanimous consent. You do not get anywhere that way.

It is also very important that the general impatience not provoke us into deceiving ourselves. We have many difficulties in store for us. The stability of relationships in society, the reliability of customary forms of public life have value in themselves, and it is going to seem painful to many people to break them up. Time will be needed to form new relationships in society, and during this period old problems will usually be made more acute, and many new ones will arise.

The results of the "trial-and-error method," which can't be avoided in restructuring, will be felt by many social groups, but perhaps primarily by administrative workers. It is already considerably harder for them than in the past, and it will probably get still worse.

Q. Do you think that restructuring will be dragged out over a long period?

In principle, two variants are possible—either a rapid and radical reform or a long-drawn-out and gradual one. Both of these have their dangers.

The first of these is not without serious risk, since, as I have already said, there is not as yet complete clarity, a profound scientific interpretation, or a unified model of the transitional period and of the results of restructuring. There is one other danger: the process of democratization itself may be bureaucratized to the point of outright negation. Remember what the collective contract was turned into during the process of mass dissemination of this essentially good idea.

On the other hand, if the matter is excessively drawn out the loss of stability of life in society may provoke increasing discontent among people, and in that case, not only temporary retreats but an extended abandonment of the reform are possible. The experience of the Hungarian reform of the 1980s, in which individual, narrow changes were introduced into the economic mechanism gradually, has shown that this method does not permit a qualitative change in the system of management of the economy. And, after all, economic transformations are the basis for other transformations in society.

Q. How, in your opinion, should the reform be conducted?

I think that all its main problems should first be worked out in a profound, scientific, and comprehensive way, and that a solidly based conception should be formed that would embrace all basic elements of the model. Then the reform should be put through relatively quickly—perhaps in one or two years, simultaneously and comprehensively.

But this is no more than a hypothesis. In actuality, the strategy has to be chosen by relying not only on theory, but also on the broadest kind of socioeconomic studies which would permit us to understand and take account of the position, interests, opinions, and behavior of all social groups.

Q. What do you yourself call restructuring?

A return to the path of the building socialism in full measure. At the end of the 1920s we took a detour and ended up in a "pre-crisis situation." Now we have to restore what we lost.

Q. What, exactly?

The habit of regarding public property as our own, and the active involvement of each person in the life of society. I think that a deeply thought-out and extremely serious return to the Leninist cooperative plan, which we have not implemented, can play a huge role here. Of course, under new conditions the cooperative movement may not look the way it did in the 1920s, but it seems to me that it remains even now one of the best schools of socialist management.

Q. We have many collective farms, and this is cooperative property, but I do not see any great difference between them and state enterprises.

Right now, in most cases there is no difference, and the very idea of cooperation has been distorted in these farms. The collective farms are run by government officials, even down to the smallest detail. These farms, in turn, ask "uncle" for everything they need. Now in the

Hungarian agricultural and consumers' cooperatives with which I am familiar, no one has to be "brought in" to participate in management: all members of the cooperative participate in it without that. What flexibility, what skillful organization of work! But the main thing is an absolutely natural attitude of all members of the cooperative to their common property and activity as something that is theirs. That is real socialism.

I am convinced that socialism does not by any means presuppose only the state form of property; neither cooperative nor even private property, within definite limits, is contradictory to it. We need a greater variety of forms of economic life and a greater degree of democracy in the life of society. And although not all our current problems are reducible to this, it is one of the main ones.

Interview conducted by I. Pruss.

APPENDIX | The Novosibirsk Report

EDITOR'S NOTE: *In the summer of 1983 several Western newspapers carried excerpts from a confidential paper said to have been prepared by T. I. Zaslavskaia for presentation at a seminar held under the auspices of the CPSU Central Committee, the USSR Academy of Sciences, and Gosplan. The full text of the paper, commonly referred to as The Novosibirsk Report, was published in English translation in the British journal* Survey. *Insofar as we can tell, the Report—in the form in which it appears here—has not been published in the Soviet Union. Just how a paper presented at a "closed" Soviet seminar reached the West remains unclear.*

The common assumption that Zaslavskaia was the author of the Report is certainly reinforced by comparing it with articles published under her name in the Soviet Union in 1984–85 (see selections 2–4 above). The Report is a significant historical document on at least two counts. It illustrates some of the reformist proposals and concepts presented by scholars to Soviet political leaders in the early 1980s. It also demonstrates that papers that were apparently too "bold" to publish in 1983 seem relatively "tame" in comparison with material regularly published in 1987–88 (as an illustration, compare the Report and the interview translated above).—M.Y.

1. The substantial lagging of production relations in Soviet society behind the development of its productive forces

Over a number of decades, Soviet society's economic development has been characterized by high rates and great stability. This automatically suggested a notion about the organic nature of its features for the management of a planned socialist economy. However, in the past 12–

The Novosibirsk Report was published in Volume 28, No. 1 of *Survey: A Journal of East & West Studies* and is reprinted by arrangement with *Survey*. Copyright © 1984 by *Survey*. Translated by Teresa Cherfas.

15 years a tendency toward a noticeable decline in the rate of growth of the national income began to make itself felt in the development of the economy of the USSR. If in the Eighth Five-Year Plan the average annual increase was 7.5 percent and in the Ninth it was 5.8 percent, then in the Tenth it fell to 3.8 percent, and in the first years of the Eleventh it was about 2.5 percent (with the average population growth at 0.8 percent per annum).[1] This does not provide for either the rate of growth in living standards that is required for the people, or for the intensive technical retooling of production.

Increasing effectiveness and speeding up the rate of development of the economy is of paramount concern for the party, the people, and the scientists. In their analyses of the reasons for the negative tendencies in the economy, separate groups of scientists have placed the emphasis on deterioration in conditions for mining raw minerals, the growing frequency of years of drought, the structural disproportions in the country's national economy (the falling rate of investment, deterioration of transport, insufficient interest on the part of the workers in the results of their labor, the weakness of labor discipline, and so on).

All these factors do indeed play a determined role in the creation of the tendencies under scrutiny, but they bear a particular character while the deterioration of the economic indices takes place in the majority of sectors and regions. Therefore, there is a more general reason at the foundation of this phenomenon. In our opinion, it consists in the lagging of the system of production relations, and hence of the mechanism of state management of the economy which is its reflection, behind the level of development of the productive forces. To put it in more concrete terms, it is expressed in the inability of this system to make provision for the full and sufficiently effective use of the labor potential and intellectual resources of society.

The basic features of the present system of state management of the economy of the USSR (and thus of the system of production relations to which it gives rise) were formed roughly five decades ago. Since that time, this system has repeatedly been readjusted, renewed, and improved, but not once has it undergone a qualitative restructuring which would reflect fundamental changes in the state of the productive forces.

The most important features of the system of state management of the Soviet economy, noted in the scientific literature, include: a high level of centralization in economic decisions, the character of production planning being based on direct indicators, the weak development of market relations (the prices of goods in demand and the means of production bear no relation to their social value; the centralization of supplies of materials and technology to enterprises, the absence of a market for production, and so on), the centralized regulation of all forms of material incentives for labor, the prevalence of the branch over the territorial principle of management, lack of departmental liaison in the management of the economy by branch and sub-branch, restrictions on economic rights, and consequently also on enterprises' economic responsibility for the results of their economic activity, restrictions on all aspects of informal economic activity by the population in the areas of production, services, and exchange. All these features reflect the predominance of administrative over economic methods, of centralization over decentralization.

The scientific basis of the system of economic management described above is the theoretical notion developed by economic science about the laws of social reproduction under socialism. This is partially reflected in the textbooks on political economy and in specific economic disciplines, in dictionaries of philosophy and economics, and it can partially be inferred from the actual practice of management of the national economy. The main elements in it are based on the notions:

1. that socialist production relations "outflank" the development of the productive forces, thereby ruling out any contradictions between them;

2. that there are no deep, much less antagonistic, contradictions between individual, group, and public interests under socialism, just as there are none among the interests of different classes and social groups;[2]

3. that the labor of workers in socialist production has a direct social character;

4. that, as a result of this, there is no need to affirm the social necessity for individual expenditure on the production of goods by means of the market mechanism, i.e. of the inorganic nature of commodity and monetary relations for the socialist economy;

5. of the unconditional domination of social production over all kinds of unformalized personal and group labor, the practical impossibility of "competition" between the public and private sectors in the socialist economy for labor, the working hours of the workers, the material production resources, and market outlets;

6. of the workers in socialist production as the "bearers of labor,"

the labor resources of society, the object of centralized management "from above." To the extent that the resources are by their very nature passive, to the extent that they do not act but are "utilized," do not perform actions, but "function," do not change their place of work but are "distributed" and "redistributed," so similarly one cannot expect people who are just "labor resources" to engage in activities such as, for example, participation in management, creative initiative, striving after their own ideas;

7. of the absolute predominance in people's economic activities of material needs, stimuli and incentives (in contrast to their real complex motivations, particularly the substantial role of social and spiritual motives).

The above notions, and the system of centralized (primarily by administrative means) economic management based on them, correspond for the most part to the level of development of the productive forces of Soviet society in the 1930s. The material and social base of large-scale socialist production at that time was only just beginning to take shape, and the level of real socialization of labor remained comparatively low. The links between the branches, enterprises, and regions were as yet easily "overseen" from the center and could be regulated "from above." An overwhelming number of workers in industry had only recently left their villages and had a weakly developed sense of their rights, and no claims to participation in management. For the majority of them material incentives predominated at work over social and spiritual ones. Being relatively undeveloped, they were a convenient object of management.

The range of choice of various forms of economic behavior, which corresponded to the workers' interests, was quite limited at this time. Although formally speaking there was no unemployment in the country, in many areas and branches there were hidden structural labor surpluses. Fear of losing his job and difficulties in finding a domicile hampered the worker's mobility, and firmly bound him to the enterprise. Migration of the rural population to the towns was limited by the nonexistence of passports, and, for collective-farm members, by the necessity of obtaining agreement from the *kolkhoz* general assembly. The average level of wages was only a little higher than the minimum needed to maintain a family. Therefore, the main body of workers did not have a choice between work and leisure: the majority strove to work at full capacity in order to improve the material situation of their family. They also had to put something aside "for a rainy day," inasmuch as there was no state provision for illness and old age. To all this one must add that toward the end of the 1930s virtual wartime measures of worker discipline were introduced at enterprises and establishments (you were taken to court for being late or missing work, given a prison sentence even for petty theft of public property, and so on). Such was the social system, according to whose parameters people were consistently regarded as "cogs" in the mechanism of the national economy and behaved themselves just as obediently (and passively) as machines and materials.

However, decades have passed since then, in the course of which the political and economic situation of Soviet society has radically changed. The present state of its productive forces is different from the 1930s not only quantitatively (in terms of scale), but qualitatively (in terms of new "procedures" and "generations"). The branch, departmental, and territorial structure of the national economy has become much more complex, the number of its links has grown colossally and even more its technological, economic, and social ties. The structure of the national economy long ago crossed the threshold of complexity when it was still possible to regulate it effectively from one single center. Regional, branch, and economic disproportions in the national economy of the USSR, which emerged and can be observed in the past five-year plans, are growing relentlessly; and, more than anything else, indicate the exhaustion of possibilities for centrally administered economic management, the necessity for more active use of "automatic" regulators in balancing production, linked to the development of market relations. In this situation, the scientists' tardiness in stating their position on the direct social nature of socialist labor and the "special" nature of socialist commodity and monetary relations has been a poor turn to society.

Important changes have also taken place in the social type of worker in the socialist economy. The level of his education, culture, general information, and awareness of his social position and rights, has grown incomparably. The main body of skilled workers, on whom above all the effectiveness of the production process depends, nowadays has a rather wide political and economic horizon, is able to evaluate critically the leaders' economic and political activities, accurately recognizes its own interests and can defend them if necessary. The spectrum of needs and interests of workers is today more abundant and broader than that of workers in the 1930s; moreover, in addition to economic, it includes social and spiritual needs. It testifies to the substantial increase in the level of the workers' personal development, but at the same time it is an indication that they have become a much more complex object of management than previously.

The change in the predominant social type of worker would, in turn, not have been possible without substantial changes in the socio-economic conditions of the people's sphere of activities. The democratization of political life, the broadening and constitutional bolstering of individual rights, the universal issue of passports and equalizing of civil rights for every group within the population, a sharp improvement in the standard of living, the introduction of social welfare for sickness and old age, and also the beginning of labor shortages in recent years in the majority of sectors and regions in the country—all these assisted a significant broadening of economic freedom in the workers' behavior and, as a result, the role of subjective factors in economic development increased.

Finally, there has been a qualitative change, in the course of the period in question, in the material and technical base of production and the demands made by it on human labor. The size and value of the means of production used by this labor and its technical armory have grown many times. As a result, on the one hand the level of productive labor has greatly increased, but on the other, the scale of damage inflicted upon society through careless labor, violations of labor and technology discipline, irresponsible attitudes to technology, etc., have also risen. The widespread application in many sectors of the economy of complete technological systems, the increase in the specific weight of labor given over to the functions of adjustment, control, and regulation, and improvement of technological concerns have noticeably increased the demand for qualifications, reliability, and responsibility in human labor, for workers' personal involvement in plan fulfillment, and so on. The General Secretary of the Bulgarian Communist Party described these tendencies thus: "For fruitful and effective labor it is necessary today to have modern skills, the ability to manage complex technology and technological processes, a high level of organization and discipline, individual readiness to take on responsibility and calculated risks, the ability to seek out new ideas, solutions, and new working methods."[3] In fact, man is often the weakest link in the technological chain.

The overall results of all these advances are, on the one hand, an increase in the technological demands made on the labor behavior of the workers, and on the other, a decrease in the effectiveness of centralized production management, based on the administrative regulation of the activities of the lower-ranking links by the higher. Based on the expectation of a relatively low level of development in the workers, this system appears unable to regulate the behavior of more developed (in personal terms) and economically free workers, unable to make sufficiently effective use of their labor potential and intellectual resources, unable to ensure a high level of labor, production and plan discipline, high quality work, effective use of technology, or to assure positive modes of conduct in the managers, accountants, and supply technicians.

As we see it, all this testifies to the fact that the present system of production relations has substantially fallen behind the level of development of the productive forces. Instead of enabling their accelerated development, it is becoming more and more of a brake on their progressive advancement. One outcome of this is the inability of production relations to provide modes of conduct for workers in the socioeconomic sphere that are needed by society. Let us look at this question in greater detail.

2. The production relations of socialism and the socioeconomic behavior of the workers

One of the peculiarities of our time is the significant strengthening of the role of behavioral factors in the functioning and development of the economy. The nature of the socioeconomic behavior of the workers turns out to have a decisive influence on the conditions, as well as on the effectiveness, of production. Therefore, production today can only be successfully managed if we can learn to regulate the behavior of the workers.

Socioeconomic behavior is the system of interconnected deeds and actions which are carried out by workers in the social and economic spheres of life; emanating from the workers' own interest, their goal is the satisfaction of their material, social, and spiritual needs. Reflecting the subjective aspect of human activity, this behavior bears an essential influence on its results and effectiveness.

Patterns of the workers' socioeconomic behavior are extraordinarily diverse. It is neither possible nor necessary to describe them in detail. Therefore, we shall restrict ourselves below to a brief enumeration of the most important aspects of this behavior, indicating which aspects of the economy are influenced by each one.

Demographic behavior, found in the sphere of the human reproduction, manifests itself in different groups of the population, in the customary marriage patterns for men and women, the average duration of the marriage, the terms, frequency and reasons for annulment of marriage, the number of children and the birth-rate. It would follow that within this sphere is also included the behavior associated with the length of time that the worker is able to work, his health, his longevity. The latter shows itself in the extent to which regimes of work and rest are observed, in the methods employed for preventing illness, for cures and self-administered remedies, the proliferation, on the one hand, of lessons in physical education and sport, and on the other, of bad habits (drunkenness, alcoholism, drug abuse). The peculiarities of demographic behavior bear on the general size, dynamics, age and sex composition, health and territorial distribution of the working population, of children, young people, the elderly, and the disabled.

The behavior of the population *in the sphere of education*, which manifests itself in the choice of profession, of types of general and specialized learning, of participation in various ways of raising one's qualifications, self-education and so on, is a factor in the formation of the professional and qualification structure of cadres.

Migration and mobility behavior manifests itself in the transfer of workers, stimulated by group and individual interests, between, on the one hand, different areas of employment, branches, enterprises, professions, and on the other, between regions, town and country, and between different towns and villages. The results are changes in the territorial and branch distribution of the work force and the provision of labor-supply to different parts of production.

The *professional-labor* behavior of the workers at their place of work is characterized by their relations to work, the level of discipline, the quality of work, the extent to which norms are fulfilled, by responsibility, reliability, manifestations of economic initiative, and so on. Its chief results lie in the effectiveness of production and the quality of output.

Individual economic behavior consists of the subjective aspects of the population's activities in the private sector of production: work in the private, subsidiary economy or in the collective allotments of individual apartment and employment buildings, in the pursuit of various crafts, hunting, fishing, etc. The modes of this type of behavior determine on the one hand the scale of labor costs in the private sector of production and, on the other, the volume of additional output thus created.

There are also diverse modes of behavior by people *in the spheres of distribution, exchange, and consumption.* Their influence tells primarily on the distribution of the national revenue: the relation between consumption and investment, the level and structure of income of different social groups, and so on.

Motivated by individual and group interests, the socioeconomic behavior of the workers has a substantial influence on practically all aspects of the economy and is therefore one of the sources of spontaneity in its development. The role of the spontaneous—that is, not regulated—behavior of the workers in the development of the socialist economy has many ramifications. Several aspects of it often infringe upon its planned character, cause disproportions and lower the rate of production development. But other aspects testify to the release of the workers' creative forces, to the raising of their labor activity and to making active use of social reserves in production effectiveness. The management of the workers' economic behavior is thus a complicated affair.

Within the framework of this problem, one can distinguish two tasks, each demanding a different approach. The first lies in determining, from the point of view of public interests, the optimum sphere of individual behavior for workers in each field of their socioeconomic activities which are not regulated "from above." The second task is indirectly to provide modes of socioeconomic behavior for workers, in the sphere of choice left to them, which are in line with public interests.

The determination of the first task is connected with the fact that the boundary between the activity *per se* and its subjective aspect—behavior—is not fixed. It depends on how strictly the given activity is regulated. As an example, where labor discipline is weak, the workers have the possibility of working only part of the time allocated, of being absent from work, of permitting stoppages, of drinking alcohol at their place of work, and so on. The least disciplined section of workers takes advantage of this opportunity, while the main nucleus of skilled workers works honestly. Under these conditions, the use made of work hours is an important indication of workers' behavior at work.

The introduction of order, the raising of the demand for labor discipline, the strengthening of control over the use of work hours, change the situation: the regular attendance of the workers at their place of work becomes the norm and by the same token ceases to reflect the peculiarities of their individual behavior. Today, their individual relationship to work manifests itself in the varying degrees of care and attention which they give to it and, consequently, in the uneven quality of the produced goods. Stricter regulation of the quality of output leads to a further narrowing in the scope of the workers' labor behavior, which is restricted, for example, by differences in the expenditure of raw materials, energy, goods, in different degrees of participation in management and rationalization activities, etc.

On the whole, the more strictly regulated working and economic activity is from without, the narrower the sphere of individual behavior of those who execute it, and, so it seems, the less the influence of personal behavioral factors on the development of production. But what is the actual dependency between the rigor of administrative regulation of activity and the effectiveness of the development of the economy? Is it, indeed, that the more strictly controlled the aspects of the workers' activity, the more successful its results? For a whole number of reasons, this question has to be answered in the negative.

First, the administrative regulation of labor and of other economic activities has a centralized character and, in the majority of cases, is carried out without taking into account the conditions of specific regions, sectors, and enterprises. And since these conditions vary, the practical fulfillment of regulating rules and norms runs across great difficulties in the provinces and does not always lead to favorable results.

Second, the increasing severity in regulating activity strengthens the need to observe established rules in administrative control; this is fraught with the increase of non-productive labor and deterioration of the economic indices of the enterprises. Therefore, in practice, there is often no control on a daily basis over the observation of these rules, and they are flouted. As a result, not only is the actual leeway for workers' free behavior not curtailed, but sometimes it increases noticeably. There often arises a paradoxical situation whereby the opportunity for a positive show of initiative by the workers is reduced by multiple administrative restrictions to naught, while the spectrum of antisocial modes of behavior remains rather broad.

Third, although the strengthening of the administrative regulation of activities helps the elimination of certain negative modes of behavior, it almost inevitably also leads to the undermining of creative elements of labor, a restriction on economic and technical initiatives by the workers, the deflection of their personal interests to the realm of the family, leisure pursuits, their own household, and so on. Anyway, to transfer the economy from a path of extensive development to one of intensive development can only be done in conditions where all available social reserves and all creative potential of the workers are realized.

Thus, it is in the interests of socialist society, while regulating the key aspects of the socioeconomic activity of the workers, to leave them a sufficiently wide margin of freedom of individual behavior. Hence the necessity for directing behavior itself, i.e. the subjective relationship of the workers to their socioeconomic activity. Administrative methods of management are powerless here.[4] The management of behavior can only be accomplished in an oblique fashion, with the help of incentives which would take into account the economic and social demands of the workers and would channel their interests in a direction which would be of benefit to our society. Moreover, to be able to control behavior, it is not enough to provide the correct direction for each class or social group's interests. It is necessary to aim, on the one hand, at the coordination of public, collective, and individual interests of workers "along vertical lines," and on the other, at the integration of the interests of classes and groups, which interact as it were on the "horizontal" plane.

The realization of these tasks presupposes a serious reorganization of the system of state management of the economy and especially the rejection of administrative methods of management with a high degree of centralization of economic decision-making, and the subsequent complex transition to economic methods of regulating production.

3. A strategy for perfecting production relations

The urgent need for reorganizing the system of state management of the economy was realized in theory by the party a long time ago, and this was reflected in numerous resolutions made by the party over the past decade; in particular in the resolutions of the Twenty-fourth, -fifth, and -sixth CPSU congresses, and in those of the November of 1979, October 1980, and May 1982 Plenums of the Central Committee of the CPSU. In a speech at the November (1982) Plenum of the Central Committee of the CPSU Comrade Iu. V. Andropov again stressed that "it is necessary to create conditions—economic and organizational—such that would stimulate top quality productive labor, initiative, and enterprise. And, conversely, bad work, inactivity, and irresponsibility must, in the most direct and irredeemable fashion, affect the material rewards, the work situation and the moral authority of the workers."[5]

However, while the problem is not solved, and the present system of management of the economy stubbornly retains its existing features, party documents note the necessity of decisively overcoming this. Resolutions made about this matter are slowly being realized in a compromise fashion, as though coming up against hidden opposition. In the face of this, periods of more or less successful progress in the intended direction are from time to time replaced with "ebbs"—a return to administrative methods of management which ignore the demands of economic laws.

The reasons behind this state of affairs, as they appear to us, may be separated into the ideological, the social, and the scientific. The ideological brake on the active adjustment of the principles of management of economic life is the predominance of an over-simplified notion about the mechanism for perfecting production relations under socialism. Thus, in the encyclopedia of *Political Economy*, it is noted that "the production relations in every society form a more stable [in comparison with the productive forces—T.Z.] integral system which develops according to its own individual laws; at a certain point these lag behind the productive forces and become a brake on the further progress of the workers and of the means or the technological forms of production."[6] Further on it says that in antagonistic societies the conflict between the level of development of the productive forces and the condition of production relations manifests itself in a sharpening of the class struggle. "Either there will be the beginning of period of acute socioeconomic and political shake-ups from the inside, of modification and accommodation of production relations to the new conditions of production, or there will be an era of general crisis in the present social formation and its destruction as a result of social revolution."[7]

In contradistinction, socialist society systematically "regulates the development of production relations, secures the correspondence between them and the continuously growing productive forces, thereby accelerating economic and social progress."[8] The perfection of production relations is here realized through direct change in specific economic forms, by harmonizing economic interests through various incentives, and also through change in the organizational structure of management and in economic legislation.

According to the theories developed in political economy textbooks, the perfection of production relations within a capitalist framework constitutes a social process which reflects the conflict between social classes and groups; in socialist society, however, it is essentially deprived of social content, it ceases to reflect the struggle of interests of character. This viewpoint is expressed particularly well in the latest edition of the *Dictionary of Philosophy*, where in the corresponding entry it openly affirms that under socialism there is no group interested in the preservation of outmoded production relations and therefore their perfection takes place without social conflict.[9]

In analyzing the past decades of our economic development, we must express doubt about this point of view. Such an analysis shows that the process of perfecting production relations under socialism runs a more complicated course than is commonly suggested, to the extent that the reorganization of the existing system of production relations is given over to social groups that occupy a somewhat elevated position within this system and accordingly are bound to it through personal interest.

As is well known, the kernel of the system of production relations is constituted by the prevailing form of ownership of the means of production, which takes concrete shape in management relations, direction, and usage. The system of these relations makes up the peculiarities and distinctions in the situation of different social groups, in their interests and behavior. The concrete system of management of the national economy, reflecting this or that modification in production relations, brings about a corresponding distribution of influence among social groups, central and regional economic departments, organs of regional and territorial management, ministries and associations, associations and enterprises, etc. Therefore, a radical reorganization of economic management essentially affects the interests of many social groups, to some of which it promises improvements, but to others a deterioration in their position.

By virtue of this, attempts at improving production relations, bringing them into greater correspondence with the new demands of productive forces, attempts undertaken by the higher organs of power, cannot run their course without conflict. The successful resolution of this task is only possible on the basis of a well-thought-out socialist strategy being brought into play, a strategy that would simultaneously stimulate the activity of groups interested in changing present relations and block the actions of groups capable of obstructing this change. The attempts to reorganize the management of the national economy, undertaken during the last five-year plan, did not take into consideration the social aspects of the process of improving production relations under socialism, and this was one reason, so it seems to us, for their lack of success.

The second group of reasons, which caused an inadmissible post-ponement of the transition to economic methods of management, we have called social. In this connection, we pose the question: "Which social group's interests are affected by a transition from principally administrative to primarily economic methods of management?"

In the opinion of many Soviet economists, one of the peculiarities of the present system of state management of the economy of the USSR is the relative slackening off of the functions of, on the one hand, the highest link, i.e. of the organs representing general state interests (Gosplan of the USSR and others), and on the other, of the lowest link, i.e. of the immediate producers of output—the associations and enter-prises. In contradistinction to this, the functions of the intermediate link of management—the ministries and departments (with their terri-torial organs)—patently suffer from hypertrophy. Hence the well-known slackness in the processes of economic management, the viola-tions of the proportional development of the economy, the paralyzing constraints on the economic initiatives of the labor collectives and informal groupings in the population.

Any serious reorganization of economic management must be ac-companied by a certain redistribution of rights and responsibilities among various groups of workers. Thereby, the expansion of every group's rights is, as a rule, combined with an increase of responsibil-ities; and a decrease of responsibilities goes hand in hand with a reduction of rights. Because of this, the attitude of the majority of groups to possible transformations in production relations, and to the economic mechanism which is their reflection, is not unambiguous.

Thus, a good number of workers in the central organs of manage-ment, whose prospective role ought to be increased, is afraid that its responsibilities will become substantially more complicated, as eco-nomic methods of management demand much more of highly qualified cadres than do administrative methods. The guarded response of this group of workers to the idea of a transition to and a consistent applica-tion of economic methods of management often manifests itself in unfounded assertions, as though such a transition was going to under-mine the centralized motive power in the development of the socialist economy, or to reduce the real importance of the plan.

The reorganization of production relations promises a substantial narrowing and simplification in responsibilities for workers in departmental ministries and their organs. However, it is pregnant with just as significant a reduction in their rights, in their economic influence and also in the number of their apparatuses: the liquidation of many departments, administrations, trusts, branches, etc. that have grown like mushrooms in recent decades. Naturally, such a prospect does not suit the workers who at present occupy numerous "cosy niches" with ill-defined responsibilities, but thoroughly agreeable salaries.

Logically speaking, the group which must be more interested in the transition to economic methods of management is the managerial "staff" of the enterprises (associations), whose rights it has been proposed to widen sharply, and in the second place, the ordinary workers and engineering and technical personnel, who could use their individual capabilities more fully, work more effectively and receive a higher salary. However, in practice both these groups are not homogeneous in their subjective attitude to the projected reorganization of the economic mechanism. The more qualified, energetic and active representatives of these groups reckon that they are not working at full strength now. They want to realize themselves more fully in their work, to have better living conditions, and thus they support ideas about the intensification of the economy. In contrast to this, the more apathetic, the more elderly, and the less qualified groups of workers are worried that they will have to "pay for it" if their rights are broadened and their salaries increased, with a sharp growth in their obligations, increasing labor intensity, and more economic responsibility for the results. And this is not at all to many people's taste, the more so since the system of production relations which has been in operation over the course of many decades has formed a predominantly passive type of worker, who bears witness to the famous principles of "I need no more than anybody else" and "that's no concern of mine."

From what has been said it is evident that the social necessity of improving production relations, and likewise the system of economic management thereby reflected, will not find a clear and precise echo in the interests of many social groups. Therein resides the social reason for the high stability of the rigidly centralized, predominantly administrative, system of management of the economy, whose ineffectiveness was long ago recognized by the party and reflected in its resolutions.

The third group of reasons for the phenomenon described is linked with an insufficient level of development in the social sciences, the absence there of a fully elaborated "model" for the new economic mechanism. The fact is that production relations are an integral system, all the elements of which are interconnected. This shows itself in their ability to "reject" those more effective, but qualitatively different elements of economic relations which were experimentally grafted onto them. Essentially, what we have observed over the course of past decades was a number of attempts to inculcate in the present system individual progressive methods of management, and their subsequent rejection because they did not correspond to its spirit. Analysis of the experience accumulated in a given field leads one to the conclusion that it is impossible to improve the mechanism of economic management, arrived at many years ago, by gradually replacing the more outmoded of its elements with more effective ones. Evidently, one should recognize that the discreet replacement of concrete systems of production relations in the process of the development of the communist order means that such a change will come about rather infrequently, but for that it is a complex and deep matter.

It is natural that socialist society can decide on such a serious transformation of production relations only under the influence of objective necessity, with a clearly established aim and reliable means of achieving it. We have already spoken about the first aspect of this question: there is a need for a transformation of production relations and the system of economic management, and its aims are sufficiently clear. The economic aim of the transformation lies in raising the effectiveness and rate of development of the national economy, and the social aim is in the elimination of obstacles to the social, professional, and individual development of the workers, in the formation of a genuinely socialist attitude to labor among the workers. However, the means for achieving these aims are as yet clear only in general outline, rather as directions for principles than as decisive forms of transformation to new production relations.

Today, our social sciences are not proposing an integral, internally coordinated, and concretely thought-out, detailed "model" of a system of economic management, which it would only remain to take and carry over from scientific theory into practice. It is true that a rather serious undertaking toward the building of such a system has been embraced by Soviet lawyers, economists, and sociologists. A special place is occupied in this regard by a leading research paper, from our point of view, by B. P. Kurashvili, a small fragment of which recently appeared in print,[10] and by research papers by R. O. Khalfina, M. I. Kozyr, N. P. Fedorenko, V. A. Tikhonov, I. I. Lukinov, and many other important scientists. But nonetheless our science still has no finished "model" for the new economic mechanism, and with present methods of organizing research, in principle it cannot have one.

Of course, we must remember how technical arrangements of great complexity are being projected. Special scientific collectives are established for these aims: they work on a single plan under the direction of the main designers; this provides the structural unity of the project and the coordination and linking up of all its elements. Besides, such work is carried out in the closest contact with the state organs of management, which provide the materials and financial conditions for success.

The level of complexity in the economic mechanism of economic management is many degrees higher than that of all existing technical mechanisms; yet investigations into the elaboration of a new "model" for this mechanism are made using amateurish methods. A great number of groups is at work here, groups that although formally focused on a single problem, are in fact disparate, often duplicating one another's work and, as a result of their small number, incapable of going further than the general formulation of principles, upon which the new economic mechanism must be based. The practical realization, then, of these principles, i.e. the building of a concrete mechanism of national economic management based on economic incentives, remains a matter for the future. The social aspects of reforming economic management are as yet especially weakly worked out: concrete means for coordinating public, group and personal worker interests, methods for the provision of positive forms of economic behavior, means of activating workers' participation in the management of production and society. Hence, there are new and great tasks confronting sociology, and in particular that branch of it which we are trying to develop under the name of "economic sociology." The central objects of this scientific discipline is the social mechanism of economic development. I would now like to move on to a description of this.

4. The social mechanism of socialist economic development

The "model" for production relations worked out by Soviet science, and which corresponds to the present level of development of the productive forces, must take into consideration the complications, the "multi-dimensionality," and frequently even the conflict of interests, of the groups operating in the economic structure, the regular pattern of their behavior and interdependence, the substance of their "dialogue" with the social institutions and organs of economic management. Similarly, the elaboration of a strategy for the reorganization of production relations presupposes a knowledge of the social situation, the demands, interests, and real and potential behavior of those social groups which can substantially influence the course of the transformation.

Besides, all these questions have been extraordinarily sketchily studied. We have not even uncovered the tip of the "iceberg" of socioeconomic relations, and especially of the specific features of the social situation of different branch, official, professional and territorial groups of workers (the level and sources of their income, their living conditions, the level of public services, the structure material demand and so on). Still less is known about the substance and peculiarities of the groups' socioeconomic consciousness: the nature of their value orientation, the level of development and structure of their needs, the substance and modes of expression of their interests. The most important category from the point of view of tasks at hand is that of their socioeconomic interests, which has been much more feebly worked out in Soviet science than, for example, in Hungarian.

Extremely inadequate, from our point of view, is the connection between the research carried out in economics and that in sociology: the number of serious pieces of research at the "junction" of these sciences is small. If the substance of production relations in socialism has for a long time been studied by the economists, and the peculiarities of the social structure of socialist society by the philosophers and sociologists, then the concrete social mechanism of interaction between the economic base and the social superstructure has as yet not been uncovered by anyone. In concrete terms this shows itself in the fact that the processes, the regular patterns and tendencies of economic relations, with the socially heterogeneous types of labor. As a result, neither the economic mechanism of the formation of the social structure, nor the social mechanism of the development of the economic structure, without knowledge of which the systematic perfection of society's production relations is unlikely to be made possible, are revealed.

The collective of the department of social problems at the Institute of the Economics and Organization of Industrial Production, the Siberian

Division of the USSR Academy of Sciences, strives to present the process of the development of the socialist economy as the result of the cooperation of social groups which, although connected by their relations of comradely cooperation, at the same time have different interests which are conditioned by their situation. In other words our aim is to study the social mechanism of economic development.

When we speak of such a mechanism, we have in mind a stable system of cooperation among socioeconomic groups for the production of human life, the use of the natural environment, the creation and consumption of material wealth and services; a system on the one hand regulated by historically formed social institutions and, on the other, by the current activities of the state organs of economic management. The socioeconomic behavior of the groups, conditioned by their situation and their interests, is reflected in the specific form of functioning of the system. Providing the connection between the economic and social spheres of society, the social mechanism of economic development assures a systematic raising of production relations to the level of productive forces. The moving force of this mechanism is the contradiction between the level of development of productive forces and the state of production relations, which finds concrete expression in the interests of the socioeconomic groups.

The central organs of state management of economic and social development represent the interests of society as a whole. In order to fulfill their functions, they work out a concrete strategy for developing the economy and the social structure, they shape and improve the economic mechanism and directly administer the development of production.

The activities of the state organs of management form the economic and legal conditions for the behavior of the socioeconomic groups. In conjunction with this, these groups enjoy full rights as participants in the "dialogue" with the organs of economic management. Even under the strictest regimentation of behavior in the economic sphere of the population's activity, as has already been noted, there remains a definite choice of responses to the restrictions imposed by the state, responses which are often far from understood and not always realized. Hence the possibility of open and concealed conflict between group and public interests. In these cases, when the norms and rules that have been imposed (for example, restrictions on the size of private output, on fishing methods, or on the holding of more than one office, etc.) vitally affect important interests of certain groups in the population, the latter frequently search for an opportunity somehow or another of evading the prohibition and satisfying their needs. The state then takes stronger measures to suppress undesirable forms of activity, in response to which the population looks for more refined patterns of behavior which would secure the satisfaction of their interests in the new conditions, etc. In such a way, mutually oriented behavior and reciprocal influence, on the one hand by the state represented by its relevant organs of management, and on the other by the socioeconomic groups, is an important part of the social mechanism of economic development.

At the same time, the substance of this mechanism is not just reducible to the same thing as the ''dialogue'' of the population with the state, since an equally important part of it consists of groups' interaction with one another. In those cases when the interests of separate groups coincide, they usually unite for the joint achievement of their goal. If group interests are disparate, which very often happens, the possibility of conflict then arises. Some are resolved spontaneously by way of seeking out compromise forms of behavior, satisfying both sides. When a successful compromise is not reached, and the clash of group interests takes on a sharp form and receives wide publicity, the resolution of conflict is achieved with the help of appropriate arbitrators, provided, as a rule, by organs of the party and the state, who set up certain norms of socioeconomic behavior for the two sides.

As our investigations show, the social mechanism of economic development is quite complicated. Just as the mechanism of a watch consists of a large number of interlinked springs, cogs, hammers etc., so the social mechanism of economic development consists of a multitude of individual mechanisms for socioeconomic reproduction, which although linked to one another are relatively independent. At the base of each of these mechanisms lies the specific, closed system of links regulating each separate side of socioeconomic reproduction. The elements of these mechanisms are the links between pairs of socioeconomic phenomena (for example, between the position and the interests of groups, between their interests and their behavior, between their behavior and the effectiveness of their activity, etc.).

For instance, an analysis of the social mechanism of the development of the agrarian sector in society permits one to single out such individual mechanisms of reproduction in its composition as the sociodemographic, distributive-labor, socioinfrastructural, service-employer, private-economic, sociomanagerial, and many others. Without going into a detailed description of all these mechanisms, let us stress just three factors: their great number, their concrete functional character, and their close links with one another. The latter is determined by the fact that each link between the pairs of socioeconomic phenomena as a rule forms part of several individual mechanisms of reproduction. Hence the "coupling" of these mechanisms with one another, their ability either to hand over from one to the other the pulse of development, or to "compete" for resources of one type or another and restrict one another's development.

The results of the functioning of the social mechanism of economic development can have an economic and a social aspect. In the economic sphere it determines specific rates of increase of the national income, the quality of the exploitation of the natural environment, the effectiveness of scientific-technical progress. The social results of the working of a given mechanism can be seen in the formation of a specific type of person performing economic activity: the worker (executor or manager), the recipient of profits, the buyer, the consumer.

As Karl Marx observed, the human individual is an "imprint" of all the social relations in which he is involved and has been involved. Therefore, every system of production relations forms a particular social type of economic activity, which corresponds to its essence, and first and foremost a specific type of worker. The features of this type of person are determined not by such exogenous, in relation to production relations, indicators as the age and sex composition, the professional and occupational structure, physical strength, health and so on, but by firmly adopted norms of behavior in the spheres of production, distribution, exchange and consumption. For an evaluation of the social type of worker formed by a concrete system of production relations the presence in the basic mass of them of such qualities as conscientiousness, diligence, industriousness, responsibility, reliability, discipline, the ability to take independent decisions, including calculated risks, honesty, respectability, high principles, caution and so on, is important.

One can only judge the social qualities of the workers on the basis of their behavior, which creates an impression of identity between the concepts of the "type of worker" and the "type of behavior." But the meaning of these concepts is different. The character of behavior is contingent upon opportunities and depends not only on the type of workers, but also on the other circumstances in which he finds himself at a given moment. Therefore the forms of economic behavior are more flexible and undergo far greater alterations in the face of changes in external conditions.

In contrast to this, the worker's belonging, in his individual relationship, to a certain social type is a factor of lasting effect, the influence of which tells on the development of the economic structure not only during the course of the entire life of a given generation, but even after its departure from the historical stage, as a result of the spiritual influence of older generations on newer ones. Hence the historical continuity of the specific characteristics of various national groups of workers (for example, the Russians, the Georgians, the Estonians, the Germans), each of which as it were bears the imprint of the path of development of those nations over the course of centuries. As far as the social type of worker that prevails in every period appears to be the result not only of present, but also of earlier existing social relations, to that extent does it command great momentum and does not give itself up easily to coercion by the administrative organs.

However, the tenacity of the workers' social attitudes does not remove the necessity for their purposeful formation by socialist society, first and foremost by way of perfecting the social mechanism of economic development. For although this mechanism is not capable of changing the existing type of worker as is necessary in the short term, the results achieved in this respect positively affect economic development in the long run and have substantial influence on the development of society as a whole.

In the light of what has been said, we must admit that the social mechanism of economic development as it functions at present in the USSR does not ensure satisfactory results. The social type of worker formed by it fails to correspond not only to the strategic aims of a developed socialist society, but also to the technological requirements of contemporary production. The widespread characteristics of many workers, whose personal formation occurred during past five-year plans, are low labor- and production-discipline, an indifferent attitude to the work performed and its low quality, social passivity, a low value attached to labor as a means of self-realization, an intense consumer orientation, and a rather low level of moral discipline. It is enough to mention the broad scale of activity of the so-called "touts," the rampant spread of various "shady" deals made at public expense, the development of illegal output, of irregular registrations, of procuring wages which are not dependent on the results of labor.

It is our conviction that both the expansion of these negative phenomena and the lowering of the rate of growth of production come about as a result of the degeneration of the social mechanism of economic development. At present, this mechanism is "tuned" not to stimulate, but to thwart the population's useful economic activity. Similarly, it "punishes" or simply cuts short initiatives by the chiefs of enterprises, in the sphere of production organization, aiming at the improvement of economic links. Nowadays, higher public value is placed not on the activities of the more talented, brave and energetic leaders, but on the performances of the more "obedient" chiefs, even if they cannot boast production successes.

An important source of social tension in the economic structure is not only the "inharmoniousness," but also the clash of interests between vertically aligned groups: between workers and foremen; foremen and the chiefs of enterprises; chiefs of enterprises and administrators in the ministries.

Finally, the centralized system of rules and norms of economic activity, which was created over the course of decades, has now become tangled to an unbelievable degree and many of its elements have become outdated. The "economic labyrinth," called upon to direct the workers' behavior in the channel needed by society, actually consists of a multitude of "saps" and "manholes," which allows the achievement of the same income by a significantly easier route. This extensively promotes not only undesirable practices, but also the formation of a type of worker who is alien to genuinely socialist values.

The solution to actual problems of Soviet economic development is closely connected with the perfection of the social mechanism of its development. It is precisely here that the more complex problems are concentrated today, and it is precisely from here that we should begin work on overcoming the negative tendencies in the economic life of the country.

But in order to put the social mechanism of economic development "in for repair," it is necessary to study it, to understand its internal structure, expose its weak points and establish ways of strengthening them. A new branch of science—economic sociology—must take upon itself the resolution of these tasks. The object of its investigations is the interaction of the economic and social spheres of society, of economic and social processes, including the definition of economic conditions for achieving social aims, analysis of the social factors in economic development, and the prognosis for its social results. The following points make up the picture of the system of scientific tasks in this regard:

1. The study of the economic structure of society, that is the analysis of social groups distinguished essentially by their position in the economic sphere, their place and role in the development of the economic structure, the level and source of their income. In comparison with the social, the economic structure of society is more concrete: it embraces not only class, but territorial, departmental, professional, official, salaried and other groups. Analysis of this structure presupposes an investigation into its quantitative "incompleteness," into the socioeconomic positions within it, and also into the links and interaction between opposite groups of workers.

2. Investigation into the social self-awareness of economic groups—their value orientations, needs, interests, motives for activity. The social typology of members of society according to the modes and motivation for their behavior in the economic sphere. Clarification of the most important factors which form the various social types of worker, of possibilities for and ways of directing this process.

3. Analysis of the concrete regular patterns of behavior of economic groups in the social sector of production, in the private and domestic economy, in the spheres of production, distribution and exchange. Clarification of the dependence of forms of behavior on the social qualities of the subjects (workers, consumers, and so on) on the one hand, and on the socioeconomic conditions for activity, on the peculiarities of the existing economic system, on the other.

4. Study of the forms, conditions and results of the interaction of organs of economic administration with economic groups. Analysis of the practice of state regulation of economic activity and of the behavior of groups, of their reactions to state controls, of changes in their behavior under the influence of altered economic and labor legislation, of new economic regulations, etc.

5. The establishment and elaboration of methods for integrating

the interests of economic groups, between the groups themselves and with the interests of society, of fuller and more effective use of the human factor in production at all levels and in all links of the economic system. In such cases where it is possible, there should be experimental checking of the more progressive forms of social and economic relations.

6. In conjunction with other scientific disciplines (political economy, law, social psychology, cybernetics) there should be the establishment, elaboration and practical examination of an integral "model" for the social mechanism of economic development, based on the economic mechanism, with effective feedback which would ensure the intensive development of production in the first place, and, secondly, the formation of a genuinely socialist type of worker.

*   *   *

We have examined but a few of the problems connected with the need for and ways of mobilizing social reserves for the development of the socialist economy. In fact, the spectrum of problems in this field is broad and varied. But enough has been said to draw the attention of participants in this scientific seminar to the questions that we would like to put forward for discussion.

Notes

1. Data from the report on *The National Economy of the USSR in 1981* (Statistika, Moscow), 1983.

2. A thoroughly convincing critique of these positions is given in A. P. Butenko's article "Protivorechiia razvitiia sotsializma kak obshchestvennogo stroia" (Contradictions in the development of socialism as a social order) in *Voprosy filosofii*, 1982, No. 10, pp. 20–27.

3. Todor Zhivkov, Report at the Plenum of the Central Committee of the Bulgarian Communist Party, 19 April 1982. "Osnovnye polozheniia partiinoi kontseptsii novogo Kodeksa o trude" (Basic propositions in the party conception of the new Codex on labor) in *Rabotnichesko delo*, 3 December 1982.

4. A great number of interesting and quite concrete ideas about methods of regulating the labor behavior of the workers with the help of economic controls were expressed in comrade T. Zhivkov's report at the November (1982) Plenum of the Central Committee of the Bulgarian Communist Party (see the newspaper *Rabotnichesko delo* of 3 December 1982).

5. *Pravda*, 23 November 1982.

6. Iu. A. Vasil'chik, "Sootvetstviia proizvodstvennykh otnoshenii kharakteru i urovniu razvitiia prolzvoditel'nykh sil zakon" (Law of correspondences of production relations to the character and level of development of productive forces) in the encyclopedia *Political Economy* (Moscow, 1979), vol. 3, p. 589.

7. Ibid., p. 589.

8. L. I. Abalkin, "Proizvodstvennye otnosheniia" (Production relations), ibid., pp. 273–274.

9. L. I. Abalkin, "Zakon sootvetstviia proizvodstvennykh otnosheniia kharakteru i urovniu razvitiia proizvoditel'nykh sil" in *Filosofskii slovar'* (Moscow, 1980), p. 116.

10. B. P. Kurashvili, "Gosudarstvennoe upravlenie narodnym khoziaistvom: perspektivy razvitiia" (State management of the national economy: perspectives for development) in *Sovetskoe gosudarstvo i pravo*, No. 6, 1982, pp. 38–48.

INDEX

ABOUT THE
AUTHOR AND
THE EDITOR

TAT'IANA I. ZASLAVSKAIA, born in Kiev in 1927, was trained in economics at Moscow State University and at the Institute of Economics of the USSR Academy of Sciences. In 1963 she joined the staff of the Institute of the Economics and Organization of Industrial Production at the Siberian branch of the Academy of Sciences, where she has headed the Social Problems Department for twenty years. She was elected president of the Soviet Sociological Association in 1986 and recently was appointed director of a newly formed Center for the Study of Public Opinion on Socioeconomic Issues. Zaslavskaia is the author and editor of many published works, most recently *Social and Economic Development of the Siberian Countryside* (in Russian; 1987) and (with R. V. Ryvkina) *The Sociology of Economic Life* (in Russian; forthcoming). She is also the editor of the Soviet journal *Economics and Applied Sociology*.

MURRAY YANOWITCH is professor emeritus of economics at Hofstra University in Hempstead, NY. He is the author of numerous works about Soviet social, economic, and labor issues including *Social and Economic Inequality in the Soviet Union* (1979) and *Work in the Soviet Union* (1985) and he edited the volumes *Social Stratification and Mobility in the USSR* (with Wesley A. Fisher; 1973), *Soviet Work Attitudes: The Issue of Participation in Management* (1979), and *The Social Structure of the USSR* (1986). He is also the editor of the translation journals *Problems of Economics* and *Soviet Sociology*.